Alexander James Dallas

Features of Mr. Jay's Treaty

To which is annexed a view of the Commerce of the United States, as it

stands at Present, and as it is fixed by Mr. Jay's treaty

Alexander James Dallas

Features of Mr. Jay's Treaty
To which is annexed a view of the Commerce of the United States, as it stands at Present, and as it is fixed by Mr. Jay's treaty

ISBN/EAN: 9783337192372

Printed in Europe, USA, Canada, Australia, Japan

Cover: Foto ©ninafisch / pixelio.de

More available books at **www.hansebooks.com**

FEATURES

OF

Mr. *JAY's* TREATY.

TO WHICH IS ANNEXED

A View of the Commerce of the
UNITED STATES,

AS IT

STANDS AT PRESENT, AND AS IT IS FIXED BY

Mr. JAY's TREATY.

PHILADELPHIA:
PRINTED FOR MATHEW CAREY, BY LANG & USTICK.
1795.

CONTENTS.

[FROM THE AMERICAN DAILY ADVERTISER.]

Messrs. Dunlap & Claypoole,

THE following Sketch of " The Features of Mr. Jay's Treaty," was made, originally, with a view to ascertain, for private satisfaction, the principles and operation of an Instrument, which has excited such extensive curiosity, and is calculated to produce such important effects. It is published, however, at the instance of several persons, who think that the subject should be placed in every possible light ; and that no citizen can be justified at this crisis, in suppressing his opinions, or in withholding his share of information from the common stock. But while it is committed to the press, I wish it to be considered merely as a text, which may hereafter be extended by commentary, or explained by illustration ; and though it will give me pleasure (since my sole object on this occasion is the investigation of political truth) to see it become a source of candid animadversion, I trust it will not, according to the custom of contending parties, be regarded as an instrument of faction, nor be made the foundation of slander and abuse.

FEATURES

OF

Mr. Jay's Treaty.

I. *The origin and progress of the negociation for the Treaty, are not calculated to excite confidence.*

1. THE administration of our government have, seemingly at least, manifested a policy favourable to Great Britain, and adverse to France.

2. But the house of representatives of Congress, impressed with the general ill conduct of Great Britain towards America, were adopting measures, of a mild, though retaliating nature, to obtain redress and indemnification. The injuries complained of were, principally, 1st. The detention of the western posts—2dly. The delay in compensating for the negroes carried off at the close of the war—and 3dly, The spoliations committed on our commerce. The remedies proposed, were, principally, 1st. The commercial regulations of Mr. Madison—2dly. The non-intercourse proposition of Mr. Clarke—3dly. The sequestration motion of Mr. Dayton—4thly. An embargo—and 5thly, Military preparation.

3. Every plan of the legislature was, however, suspended, or rather annihilated, by the interposition of the executive authority ; and Mr. *Jay*, the chief Justice of the United States, was taken from his judicial seat, to negociate with Great Britain, under the influence of

the prevailing fentiment of the people, *for the redrefs of our wrongs.* Query—Are not his commiffion and the execution of it, at variance? Is any one of our wrongs actually redreffed? Is not an atonement to Great Britain, for the injuries which fhe *pretends* to have fuffered, a preliminary ftipulation?

4. The political dogma of Mr. Jay are well known; his predilection, in relation to France and Great Britain, has not been difguifed; and even on the topic of American complaints, his reports, while in the office of fecretary for foreign affairs, and his adjudications while in the office of chief juftice, were not calculated to point him out as the fingle citizen of America, fitted for the fervice in which he was employed. Query—Do not perfonal feelings too often dictate and govern the public conduct of minifters? But whatever may have been his perfonal difqualifications, they are abforbed in the more important confideration of the apparent violence committed by Mr. Jay's appointment, on the effential principles of the conftitution. That topic, however, has already been difcuffed, and we may pafs to the manner of negociating the treaty in England, which was at once obfcure and illufory. We heard of Mr. Jay's diplomatic honours; of the royal and minifterial courtefy which was fhewn to him, and of the convivial boards to which he was invited: but, no more! Mr. Jay, enveloped by a dangerous confidence in the intuitive faculties of his own mind, or the inexhauftible fund of his diplomatic information, neither poffeffed nor wifhed for external aid; while the Britifh negociator, befides his own acquirements, entered on the points of negociation, fraught with all the auxiliary fagacity of his brother minifters, and with all the practical knowledge of the moft enlightened merchants of a commercial nation. The refult correfponds with that inaufpicious ftate of things. Mr. Jay was driven from the ground of an injured, to the ground of an agreffing, party; he made atonement for imaginary wrongs, before he was allowed juftice for real ones; he converted the *refentments* of the American citizens (under the impreffions of which he was avowedly fent to England) into *amity and concord;* and feems to have been fo anxious to rivet a commercial chain about the neck of America, that he even forgot, or difregarded, a principal item of her own produce, (cotton) in order to make a fweeping facrifice to the infatiable appetite of his maritime antagonift. But the idea of the treaty, given by Mr. Pitt in anfwer to Mr. Fox, who, before he had feen, applauded it as an act of liberality and juftice towards America, was the firft authoritative alarm to our interefts and our feelings. "When the treaty is laid before the parliament (faid the minifter) you will beft judge whether any improper conceffion has been made to America!"

5. The treaty being fent here for ratification, the Prefident and the Senate purfue the myfterious plan in which it was negociated. It has been intimated, that till the meeting of the fenate, the inftrument was not communicated even to the moft confidential officers of the government: and the firft refolution taken by the fenate, was to ftop the lips and ears of its members againft every poffibility of giving

or receiving information. Every man, like Mr. Jay, was presumed to be inspired. In the course of the discussion, however, some occurrences flashed from beneath the veil of secrecy; and it is conjectured that the whole treaty was, at one time, in jeopardy. But the rhetoric of a minister (not remarkable for the *volubility of his tongue*) who was brought post-haste from the country ; the danger of exposing to odium and disgrace the distinguished American characters, who would be affected by a total rejection of the treaty ; and the feeble, but operative, vote of a member transported from the languor and imbecility of a sick room, to decide in the senate a great national question, whose merits he had not heard discussed ; triumphed over principle, argument and decorum !

6. But still the treaty remains *unratified ;* for, unless the British government shall assent to suspend the obnoxious twelfth article, (in favour of which, however, many *patriotic* members declared their readiness to vote) the whole is destroyed by the terms of the ratification : and if the British government shall agree to add an article allowing the suspension, the whole must return for the reconsideration of the senate. But the forms of mystery are still preserved by our government ; and attempts to deceive the people have been made abroad, upon a vain presumption, that the treaty could remain *a secret*, till it became obligatory as *a law*.

For instance, in *Fenno's* paper of the 25th of June, it is unequivocally declared, " the treaty of amity, commerce and navigation, was ratified yesterday by the Senate of the United States ; and, even while he corrects that mistake in the paper of the following day, he commits *an error* of a more extraordinary kind (particularly when we consider that he is the confidential person, who printed the treaty for the use of the senate) by asserting, that in the twelfth article, " the United States are prohibited from exporting to Europe from the said states, sugar, coffee, cotton and cocoa, *the produce of any of the West India islands.*" The fact must have been known to Mr. Fenno, that the prohibition operates universally ; whether the prohibited articles are the produce of the West India islands, of the East Indies, of the United States, or of any other part of the world. The next essay to render the envelopements of the treaty still more opaque, appeared in the American Daily Advertiser, of the 27th of June. The writer (who is said to be a member of the Senate) likewise regards the ratification, in his introduction, as a perfect one ; and after giving a gloss to the general texture of the treaty, he ascribes the obnoxious principle of the twelfth article, *to an error which, it appears, has been inadvertently introduced.* An error inadvertently introduced into an instrument, which was under the consideration of the chief justice of the United States, and the British minister, for a term of eight months ! and introduced too, into a part of that very article, which is made the sole foundation of the whole commercial superstructure !! Whenever the twelfth article ceases, the treaty declares every other article, except the ten first articles, shall also cease ! But the author of that sketch proceeds one step further—he says, " that *every cause of offence or collision* towards the French, seems to have been studiously avoided, in the progress of the negociation ;" for, " no article of the treaty *clashes in the smallest degree*, with the obligations and engagements contracted with that gallant nation !" Let the treaty speak for itself—it is more to be hoped than expected, that the voice of France should not likewise be heard in opposition to so bold an assertion.

II. *Nothing is settled by the Treaty.*

1. The western posts are *to be given up*.
2. The northern boundary of the United States is *to be amicably settled*.
3. The river meant by St. Croix river in the treaty, is *to be settled*.
4. The payment for spoliations is *to be adjusted and made*.
5. The ultimate regulation of the West India trade is to depend on a negotiation *to be made* in the course of two years after the termination of the existing war.
6. The question of neutral bottoms making neutral goods is *to be considered* at the same time.
7. The articles that may be deemed contraband, are *to be* settled at the same time.
8. The equalization of duties laid by the contracting parties on one another, is *to be hereafter treated of*.
9. All the commercial articles depend on the existence of the twelfth article, which may continue twelve years, if it is so agreed within two years after the expiration of the war ; but if it is not so agreed, it expires, and with it all the dependent parts of the treaty. Query—Does not the Senate's suspension of the twelfth article bring us to the same ground ?
10. The whole business of Mr. Jay's negociation is left open by the twenty-eighth article, for alteration, amendment and addition, by new articles, which, when agreed upon and ratified, *shall become a part of this treaty*.

Query—Does not the history of treaties prove, that whenever commissioners have been appointed by the parties, to take all the subjects of their dispute *ad referendum*, for the sake of getting rid of an immediate pressure, and patching up a peace, the matter terminates in *treating*, not in *settling* differences ?

III. *The Treaty contains a colourable, but no real, Reciprocity.*

1. The second article provides for the surrender of the western posts in June, 1796; but it stipulates, that in the mean time, the citizens of the United States shall not settle within the precincts and jurisdiction of those posts; that the British settlers there shall hold and enjoy all their property of every kind, real and personal ; and that when the posts are surrendered, such settlers shall have an election

either to remain British subjects, or to become American citizens. Query—Were not the western posts, and all their precincts and jurisdiction, the absolute property of the United States by the treaty of peace? Query—What equivalent is given for this cession of the territory of the United States to a foreign power? Query—How far do the precincts and jurisdiction of the posts extend? Query—Does not the treaty give an implied assent to major Campbell's claim, by adopting its language, as far as the falls of the Miami, and to the northern claim upon the territories of New-York and Vermont?

2. The third article stipulates that the two contracting parties may frequent the ports of *either party*, on the eastern banks of the Mississippi. Query—What ports has Great Britain on the eastern banks of the Mississippi?

3. The third article likewise opens an amicable intercourse on the lakes; but excludes us from their sea-ports, and the limits of the Hudson's bay company; and excludes them from navigating our Atlantic rivers, higher than the highest port of entry in each. Query —What are the limits of the Hudson's bay company? Query—What equivalent do the United States obtain for the general freedom of navigation, portage and passage? For it must be remembered, that the British rivers penetrate the heart of the country, but of those we can take no advantage; while Great Britain is in fact admitted to all the advantages of which our Atlantic rivers are susceptible.

4. The sixth and seventh articles provide for satisfying every demand which Great Britain has been able, at any time, to make against the United States (the payment of the British debts due before the war, and the indemnification for vessels captured within our territorial jurisdiction) but the provision made for the American claims upon Great Britain, is not equally explicit or efficient in its terms, nor is it co-extensive with the object. Query—Why is the demand for the negroes, carried off by the British troops, suppressed, waved, or abondoned? The preamble to the treaty recites an intention to *terminate the differences* between the nations: was not the affair of the negroes a difference between the nations? and how has it been terminated?

5. The ninth article stipulates, that the subjects of Great Britain and the citizens of the United States, respectively, who now hold lands within the territories of either nation, shall hold the lands in the same manner as natives do. Query—What is the relative proportion of lands so held? Query—The effect to revive the claims of British subjects, who, either as traitors or aliens, have forfeited their property within the respective states? Query—The operation of such a compact on the internal policy of the union, combined with the solemn recognition of a colony of British subjects, professing and owing allegiance to the British crown, though settled within the acknowledged territory of the United States, by virtue of the second article?

6. The tenth article declares, that neither party shall sequester or confiscate the debts or property in the funds, &c. belonging to the

citizens of the other, in cafe of a war, or of national differences. Great Britain has fleets and armies; America has none. Query— Does not this, fupported by other provifions, which forbid our changing the commercial fituation of Great Britain, or impofing higher duties on her than on other nations, deprive the United States of their beft means of retaliation and coercion? Query—Is it not taking from America her only weapon of defence; but from Great Britain the leaft of two weapons which fhe poffeffes? What is the relative proportion held by the citizens of the contracting nations, refpectively, in the funds, &c. of each other.

7. The twelfth article opens to our veffels, not exceeding feventy tons, an intercourfe with the Britifh Weft India iflands, during the prefent war, and for two years after: but it prohibits our exporting from the United States, melaffes, fugar, cocoa, coffee, or cotton, to any part of the world, whether thofe articles are brought from Britifh, French, or Spanifh iflands, or even raifed (as cotton is) within our own territory. Query—Are veffels of feventy tons equal to maintain the moft beneficial part of our trade with the Weft Indies, the tranfportation of lumber, &c.? Query—Do we not, *in the time of war* (and the continuance of the privelege, for more than two years after the war depends on the fituation in which his majefty of Great Britain fhall then find himfelf in relation to the iflands) enjoy a greater privilege, under the temporary proclamations of the colonial governors, than this article admits? Query—Have not the articles which we are prohibited from exporting, formed, of late, a valuable part of our trade? Is not cocoa chiefly cultivated by the Spaniards? Is not cotton a ftaple of America? Is our own own confumption equal to our importation or growth of the prohibited articles? Will not the want of a vent for any furplus quantity, affect the other branches of our commerce, diminifh the demand for fhip building, and injure our agriculture? If we are now thrown out of this branch of the carrying trade, fhall we be ever able to recover it? and, in fhort, will not the lofs be of lafting detriment to all our maritime exertions?

8. The thirteenth article admits us to trade in the Britifh fettlements in the Eaft Indies: but it excludes us from any fhare in the coafting trade of that country; it forbids our penetrating the interior of the country, or holding an intercourfe with the natives, unlefs under a licenfe from the local Britifh government; and it compels us to land all the articles that are there fhipped, in the United States. Is not China the independent territory of the emperor? Is not Canton an open port acceffible to all nations? Do we not obtain there, and at independent places in the Eaft Indies with which we have, at prefent, an uninterrupted communication, tea, porcelain, nankeens, filk, &c. upon the principles of a free trade? Does not a very advantageous part of the trade in that quarter of the globe, confift in the exchange of the products and manufactures of the Eaft Indies for thofe of China, and *vice verfa?* Do not our importations of Eaft India goods far exceed our confumption? Is not the trade which we carry on with thofe goods in Europe, highly beneficial?

Are not fugar and coffee a part of our importations from India, and does not the 12th article prohibit our re-exporting them? Does our trade to Europe, founded on the previous intercourfe with India, depend on the Britifh licence; and can it be maintained, under the difadvantage of a double voyage? Are we not, every voyage, making favourable impreffions on the natives of China? Do we not participate, at prefent, in the carrying trade of that country? Does not our interett in it increafe rapidly?

9. The feveral articles that regulate the rights and priveleges of the contracting parties within their refpective territories, in cafe either of them is engaged in a war, may ceafe in two years after the prefent war is terminated, and cannot be protracted beyond twelve years. Query—Are not all thefe advantages, in effect, *exclufively favourable to Great Britain*, a principal maritime power of Europe; often engaged in wars; and interefted to obtain for her fhips, her colonies, and herfelf, the ports and fupplies of this extenfive continent?

Is it probable that, during the longett poffible exiftence of this treaty (twelve years) America will be engaged in maritime wars, will want Englifh ports as a refuge for men of war, or as a retreat for prizes? Or that it will, during that period, be of importance to her objects, to prevent her enemies from arming in Englifh ports, or felling their prizes there?

10. The twenty-fecond article provides for fhips of war being hofpitably treated in the ports of the refpective contracting parties; and that officers fhall be treated with the refpect that is due to the commiffions which they bear. Query—Could not the principle of reciprocity, as well as humanity, fuggeft to Mr. Jay, that fome provifion fhould be made to protect our citizen failors from the fangs of Britifh prefs-gangs in England; and from the horrors of their prifon-fhips in the Weft Indies? Were the commiffions of his Britannic majefty of more regard than the liberties of American freemen? Or, was it unknown, that thoufands of our failors have been occafionally enflaved by the imprefs tyranny of the Britifh government? Or, that thoufands have loft their lives in noxious prifons, while their veffels were carried into Britifh ports for " LEGAL ADJUDICATION?"

11. The fourteenth article provides for a perfect liberty of commerce and navigation, and for the accommodation of traders; but fubject always to the laws and ftatutes of the two countries refpectively: Query—Are not the laws and ftatutes of England infinitely more rigid, on the fubjects of this article, than the laws and ftatutes of America?

IV. *The Treaty is an Inftrument of Party.*

1. The difcuffions, during the feffion of Congrefs in which Mr. Jay's miffion was projected, evinced the exiftence of two parties, upon the queftion, whether it was more our interett to be allied with the republic of France, than with the monarchy of Great Britain. Query—Does

not the general complexion of the treaty decide the queſtion in favour of the alliance with Great Britain? Query—Whether that complexion does not manifeſtly ariſe from the proviſions, for admitting a Britiſh colony within our territory, in the neighbourhood of the weſtern poſts; for admitting the whole Britiſh nation, without an equivalent, into a participation of our territory on the eaſtern bank of the Miſſiſſippi; for naturalizing all the holders of lands; for opening a general intercourſe with their traders on the lakes, in the interior of our country, rendering (as it is idly ſaid) the local advantages of each party common to both; for regulating the external trade of the two nations with each other; for admitting citizens to be puniſhed as pirates, who take commiſſions, &c. from a belligerent power, adverſe to either contracting party; for fettering the operations of our treaty with France; for ſurrendering criminals, &c. &c. &c.

2. The meaſures propoſed by one party to retaliate the injuries offered by Great Britain to our territorial, commercial and political rights, were oppoſed by the other, preciſely as the treaty oppoſes them. For inſtance:—

(1.) Mr. Madiſon projects a regulation of our commerce with Great Britain, by which the hoſtile ſpirit of that nation, might be controuled on the footing of its intereſt. The treaty legitimiſes the oppoſition, which was given to the meaſure in Congreſs, by declaring in article fifteen, " that no other or higher duties ſhall be paid by the ſhips or merchandiſe of the one party, in the ports of the other, than ſuch as are paid by the like veſſels or merchandiſe of all other nations; nor ſhall any other or higher duty be impoſed in one country on the importation of any articles of the growth, produce, or manufactures of the other, than are, or ſhall be, payable on the importation of the like articles of the growth, &c. of any foreign country.

(2.) Mr. Clarke propoſes to manifeſt and enforce the public reſentment, by prohibiting all intercourſe between the two nations. The treaty deſtroys the very right to attempt that ſpecies of national denunciation, by declaring in the ſame article, that " no prohibition ſhall be impoſed on the exportation or importation of any articles to or from the territories of the two parties reſpectively, which ſhall not equally extend to all other nations."

(3.) But Mr. Dayton moves, and the houſe of repreſentatives ſupport his motion, for the ſequeſtration of Britiſh debts, &c. to enſure a fund for paying the ſpoliations committed on our trade. The treaty (without regarding the reſpect due to the commiſſion which is borne by our members of Congreſs) not only deſpoils the government of this important inſtrument to coerce a powerful, yet intereſted adverſary into acts of juſtice, but enters likewiſe into a commentary, which, conſidering the conduct of one of the branches of our legiſlature, Lord Grenville, conſiſtently with decorum, could not have expreſſed, or at leaſt, Mr. Jay, for the ſake of our national dignity, ought not to have adopted. The tenth article declares, that " neither the debts due from individuals of the one nation to individuals of the other, nor fhares nor monies which they may have in the public funds, or in the public or private banks, fhall ever, in any event of war or national difference, be fequeftered or confifcated, *it being unjuft and impolitic*, that debts and engagements contracted and made by individuals having confidence in each other and in their refpective governments, fhould ever be deftroyed or impaired by national authority on account of national differences and difcontents." The terms are very fimilar to thofe that gave Mr. Dayton offence in a fpeech pronounced by Mr. Ames; and certainly it will be deemed no mitigation, that the charge of committing " *an unjuft and impolitic* act," has been wantonly engrafted upon the moft folemn of all inftruments, —a public treaty! Query:—Would Lord Grenville have confented to brand his Royal Mafter with the title of *Great Sea Robber*, if Mr. Jay's urbanity could have permitted him to borrow the epithet from another member of Congrefs, in order to infert it, in the article that relates to the Britifh fpoliations on our trade? But perhaps, Mr. Jay forgot, that the commentary operated as a reflection on the government of the United States, and only meant it as a reproach to Great Britain, for fequeftering during the late war, and retaining at this moment, the property belonging to Maryland, lying in the bank of England. It might, likewife, be intended as a fatire upon the parliamentary fequeftration of French property in the famous " Intercourfe Act:" or, perhaps, Mr. Jay anticipated the revolution in Holland, and defigned his commentary as a warning againft the feizing of Dutch property, public and private; which, however, has fince taken place, in fpite of his folemn admonition.

3. The trials that had occurred relative to the equipment of French privateers in our ports; and the enliftment of our citizens in the fervice of the republic, had produced fome embarraffment in the courfe of party purfuits. Thefe are obviated by the treaty. The Britifh nation by which the emprefs of Ruffia has always been fupplied with naval officers, and whofe fleets and armies are always crowded with volunteers from other nations, confents that her fubjects fhall not ferve againft us; and ftipulates that our citizens fhall not ferve againft her. This contract is made with a power actually engaged in a war; and feldom more than feven years clear of one; by a power at peace, not liable, from her local pofition, and political conftitution, to be involved in war, and in ftrict alliance with the nation againft whom the ftipulation will immediately operate. Captain Barney and the other Americans, who have joined the arms of France, are thus involved in the moft ferious dilemma. If they expatriate themfelves, they may poffibly efcape the vengeance of the American government; but will that fave them from the vengeance of Great Britain, whofe conceffions on the doctrine of expatriation are not quite fo liberal? By the bye, it may here be feafonably repeated, that while Mr. Jay was fo willing to prevent American citizens from *entering* into the fervice of France, he might furely have taken fome pains to fecure them from being *preffed* into the fervice of England. He would have found, on enquiry, that the in-

ftances of the latter kind are infinitely more numerous **than of** the former. But it is enough that the meafure will be introductory of a law, favourable to the view of a party which reprobates every idea of affifting the French, and cultivates every means of conciliating the Britifh.

4. It has, likewife, been thought by fome politicians, that the energies of our executive department require every aid that can be given to them, in order more effectually to **refift** and controul the popular branches of the government. Hence we **find** the treaty-making power employed in that fervice ; and Congrefs **cannot exer-**cife a legiflative difcretion on the prohibited points (though it did not participate in making the ceffion of its authority) without a declaration of war againft Great Britain. George the third enjoys by the treaty a more complete negative to bind us as ftates, than he ever claimed over us as colonies.

V. *The treaty is a violation of the general principles of neutrality, and is in collifion* **with** *the pofitive previous engagements which fubfift between America and France.*

1. It is a general principle of the law of nations, that during the exiftence of a war, neutral powers fhall not, by favour or by treaty, fo alter the fituation of one of the belligerent parties, as **to** enable him more advantageoufly to profecute hoftilities againft his adverfary. If, likewife, a neutral power fhall refufe or evade treating with one of the parties, but eagerly enter into a treaty with the other, it is a partiality, that amounts to a **breach of** neutrality. Thefe pofitions may be fupported **by the authority of the moft efteemed** writers on the fubject ; but it will **be fufficient in the prefent cafe,** to cite the conduct of Great Britain **herfelf.** Thus, **it has been** adjudged by Lord *Mansfield,* " that if a neutral fhip trades to a French colony, with all the privileges of a French fhip, *and is thus adopted and naturalized,* it muft be looked upon as a French fhip, liable to be taken." See *Judge Blackftone's reports,* 1 *vol. p.* 313, 314. According to the principle on which this judgment was given, the act of iffuing the memorable orders of the 6th of November, 1793, and the confequent feizure of all our veffels, are attempted to be juftified. Great Britain alledges (when it is injurious to **France**) **that** trading with the French iflands, *on a footing not allowed before the war,* is a breach of neutrality, and caufe of confifcation : and, therefore, Great Britain muft alfo admit, at leaft America will not deny, that trading with the Britifh iflands, on a footing not allowed before the war ; or, in different words, altering and enlarging the commercial relations of the two countries, is equally a breach of our neutrality towards France. When the fword is found to cut both ways, the party who ufes it, has no right to complain.

2. That we have, on the one hand, evaded the overtures of a treaty with France, and on the other hand, folicited a treaty from Great Britain, are facts public and notorious. Let us enquire, then,

what Great Britain has gained on the occasion, to enable her more advantageously to profecute her hoftilities againft France.

(1) *Great Britain has gained time.* As nothing is fettled by the treaty, fhe has it in her power to turn all the chances of the war in her favour; and, in the interim, being relieved from the odium and embarraffment of adding America to her enemies, the current of her operations againft France is undivided, and will of courfe flow with greater vigour and certainty. We have been for fo many years fatis-fied with *the promifes of the treaty of peace*, that Great Britain has caufe to expect, at leaft, an equal period of credit, for *the promifes of the treaty of amity.* If, indeed, it is true, that the reafons affigned by Lord Grenville to Mr. Jay, for declining an immediate furrender of the pofts, were, *firft*, that the Britifh traders might have time to arrange their out-ftanding bufinefs; *a privilege that is exprefsly granted by the treaty*, and could not therefore, furnifh a real excufe for delay; and *fecondly*, that the Britifh government might be able to afcertain what would be the probable effect of the furrender, on the Indians; *a re-fervation that demonftrates an intention to be governed by events;* we can very well account for the late extenfive fhipment of artillery and ammunition to Canada; and may eafily calculate the importance of *gaining time*, in order to promote the American, as well as European, objects of Great Britain.

(2.) *Great Britain gains fupplies for her Weft India colonies;* and *that* for a period almoft limited to the continuance of the war, under circumftances which incapacitate her from furnifhing the colonial fup-plies herfelf; and, indeed, compel her to invite the aid of all na-tions, in furnifhing provifions for her own domeftic fupport. The fupplies may be carried to the iflands either in *American* bottoms *not exceeding feventy tons*, or in *Britifh* bottoms of *any tonnage.*

(3.) *Great Britain gains an advantage over France, by prohibiting the exportation of fugar, &c.* in confequence of which the colonies of France muft, in a great meafure, remain unfupplied with provifions, &c. as they can only in general pay for them in thofe articles, *whofe ufe is confined to the American confumption.* It will be remembered, that the produce of the French iflands has of late conftituted a great part of our European remittances. If, therefore, that trade is cut off, and at the fame time, befides employing *our own fmall craft* of feventy tons, Great Britain is allowed, *to any extent of tonnage*, to be our Weft India factor, it is obvious that our confumption of fugar, coffee, &c. &c. will be abundantly fupplied, without maintaining an intercourfe with the French, or even with the Eaft Indies, to pro-cure any of thofe articles. Perhaps this method, though lefs bold, will be more effectual to prevent our furnifhing the French iflands with provifion, than declaring them to be in a ftate of blockade, and feizing the veffels that attempt to vifit them.

(4.) *It is another important gain to Great Baitain* (which might, likewife, have been adverted to under the feature of reciprocity) *that, to any extent of tonnage, her veffels may carry on the Weft India trade for us*, either to fupply our domeftic confumption, or European engagements, *subject to no other or higher duties than our own vessels*, while our own vessels are restricted to a pitiful size, and circumscribed to a particular voyage. But whatever may be thought of the benefit of acquiring for America even this scanty participation in the West India trade, no one (after the rejection of the twelfth article) will deny that the whole measure changes the relative situation of the two countries, avowedly in favour of Great Britain, and operatively injurious to France; and every such change is derogatory to our boasted neutral character.

(5.) *The admission of Great Britain to all the commercial advantages of the most favoured nation, and the restraints imposed upon our legislative independence*, as stated in the *party feature* of the treaty, are proofs of predilection and partiality in the American government, which cannot fail to improve the resources of Great Britain, and to impair the interests, as well as the attachments, of France.

(6.) *The assent to the seizure of all provision-ships*, and that, in effect, upon any pretext, at a period when Great Britain is distressed for provisions, as well as France; and when the system of *subduing by famine* has been adopted by the former against the latter nation, is clearly changing our position, as an independent republic, in a manner detrimental to our original ally. That our merchants will be paid a reasonable profit for their cargoes, &c. may render the measure more palatable to us; even under the loss of the return cargo, the derangement of the voyage, and the destruction of the spirit of commercial enterprise; but that consideration cannot render it less offensive to France. It may properly be here remarked, that Sweden and Denmark have obtained, by a spirited resistance, an actual indemnification for the seizures which have heretofore taken place, and an exemption from all such outrages in future; while America has only put those which are past, *in a train of negociation*, and has given a *legitimate effect* to those which are to come. The order, which, the English gazettes say, has recently been issued for seizing American provision-ships, on their passage to France, ought not, therefore, to be complained of, as it is merely an exercise, by anticipation, of the right granted by the treaty.

(7.) *Great Britain has gained the right of preventing our Citizens from being volunteers in the armies or ships of France!* This is not simply the grant of a new right to Great Britain, but is, at the same time, a positive deprivation of a benefit, hitherto enjoyed by France. Neither the laws of nations, nor our municipal constitution and laws, prohibited our citizens from *going to another country*, and *there*, either for the sake of honour, reward, or instruction, serving in a foreign navy, or army :—Colonel *Oswald* and many others have done it :— Captain *Barney* and many others are doing it. But a proclamation must issue to recal all such volunteers, and punishment must follow disobedience, if the twenty-first article of the treaty is to be effectuated, as the supreme law of the land.

(8.) *Great Britain has gained a right to treat and punish as pirates, any of our citizens who shall accept, even while they are in France, any commiſſion* to arm a privateer, or letter of marque. It is true, that a ſimilar proviſion is contained in other treaties; but we are now only conſidering *the alterations* which are made by the treaty under diſcuſſion, in favour of Great Britain, and injurious to France. How far there exiſts a power to define piracy, *by treaty*, will be remarked in delineating another feature of Mr. Jay's diplomatic off-ſpring.

(9.) *Great Britain has doubly gained, by obtaining in our ports, an aſylum for her ſhips of war, privateers, prizes, &c. ſtipulating for an excluſion of thoſe of her enemies, other (it is admitted) than France.* The twenty-fourth and twenty-fifth articles of the projected treaty, are nearly copied from the ſubſiſting treaty with France. It would be curious, however, to reflect on the very different motives, which muſt juſtify (if the idea of juſtification could, in the late inſtance, be at all admiſſible) theſe analogous grants. The conceſſion to France was made *when we were at war, and ſhe was not;* it was made upon a certainty of *reciprocal advantage;* and it was made *as a price* for obtaining the aid of *that gallant nation,* in the eſtabliſhment of our independence. The conceſſion is made to Great Britain *when ſhe is at war, and we are not;—without any rational proſpect of deriving any reciprocal advantage from it;* and under ſuch circumſtances of injury and inſult, as might have admoniſhed us *to reſerve it as the price for obtaining aid from other nations, in reſiſting her hoſtilities,* in-ſtead of paying it for ſmiles without affection, and promiſes without ſincerity. When we were making treaties with Holland, Pruſſia, &c. did we not expreſsly exclude them from ſuch important, and, as we have already ſeriouſly experienced, ſuch dangerous privileges?

But it will be aſked, perhaps what mighty benefit has Great Bri-tain gained, in this caſe, at the expence of France, ſince the prior ſimilar privileges of France are excluſive? *Anſwer:*—That as the privilege of Great Britain will operate againſt every other nation, it will immediately affect the French republic's alliance, offenſive and defenſive, with the United Provinces, which preceded the ratifica-tion, at leaſt, of the treaty: and it may, eventually, have the ſame pernicious influence in relation to Pruſſia, Spain and Portugal, whoſe diſpoſition to change ſides, in the preſent war, has been unequivo-cally expreſſed. Thus, though Holland and Pruſſia made treaties with us, long before Great Britain would admit the idea of a nego-ciation, and though Spain and Portugal are the only cuſtomers, who furniſh us with the ready money balance, for the very purpoſe of paying our annual accumulation of debt to Britain, the harbours of America are open to their veſſels *as prizes,* but ſhut to them as *friends:* They may be brought hither and ſold by their enemies: but if they have captured their enemy, all, but common neceſſaries, ſhall be denied to them! The habits, bias, and opinions of a people, ought not to be altogether diſregarded in making a treaty. What honeſt, feeling American, could patiently ſee an Engliſhman, *our ſunſhine ally,* bringing into our ports, *as prizes,* the ſhips of Holland, *our ally in the times that tried men's ſouls;*—a republic, indiſſolubly

united with France,—that earliest, latest, best of friends? What
honest, feeling American, even submitting to a scene so painful,
would willingly assist in expelling from our ports the ships of Holland,
which had merely retaliated, by the capture of their foe?

3. But it is time to advert to *the cases of collision* between the two
treaties; and these are of such a nature as to produce a violation of
the spirit, though not a positive violation of the words, of the previous engagements, that subsist between France and America—They
are *causes of offence, and clash in the highest degree.*

(1.) *By the ninth article of the treaty of alliance with France, we
guarantee the possessions of that nation in America.* It is true, that our
situation is such as to incapacitate, and of course to excuse us, from
a *direct* fulfilment of this guarantee; but it is equally true, that we
violate our faith, whenever we do any thing that will, either directly
or indirectly, endanger those possessions. Query—Whether facilitat-
ing the means of supplying the British forces in the West Indies, will
not be the effect of the arrangements relative to the trade with the
British islands? Query—Whether restraining our intercourse with
the French islands, as a consequence of the treaty already predicated,
will not expose them to want, and of course to the necessity of yield-
ing to their enemies? Does not every such advantage given to Great
Britain, *clash* with our engagements to France?

(2.) By our treaty with France, and indeed with several other
nations, *it is expressly stipulated, that free vessels shall make free goods.*
At the time of entering into the stipulation, and even at this moment,
the maritime strength of France (always superior to that of Denmark
and Sweden, which has, under similar circumstances, been success-
ful) could command the respect of the world for her engagments.
It is true, America neither was, nor is, in a situation to produce the
same complaisance; and, on the ground of that weakness, France
has, hitherto, candidly dispensed with a strict performance of the
treaty. But though America cannot *enforce*, she ought not to *aban-
don* her engagements: she may submit to imperious necessity, but *she
cannot voluntarily bring into question* the right of protecting, as a neutral
power, the property of France; while France is not only ready and
able to afford her property the stipulated protection, but, in confor-
mity to the stipulation, actually *allows the property of Great Britain
to pass free, under the sanction of the American flag.* When, therefore, the treaty with Great Britain *agrees*, that within two years after
the termination of the existing war, *it shall be discussed* " whether in
any, and what cases, neutral vessels shall protect enemies' property"
—*does it not clash with our previous promise to France, that free ships
shall make free goods?* And when the treaty with Great Britain, in
formal and explicit terms, *further agrees*, " that in all cases where
vessels shall be captured or detained, on suspicion of having on board
enemies' property, &c. *the part which belongs to the enemy shall be
made prize*"—Is not this *an evident collision with our previous agreement with France*, and with the security which British property enjoys
in consequence of it? While France adheres to her treaty, by per-

mitting *British goods* to be protected by American bottoms, is it honest, honourable, or confistent, on our part, *to enter voluntarily into a compact with the enemies of France*, for permitting them to take *French goods* out of our veffels? We may not be able *to prevent*, but ought we to *agree* to the proceeding? Let the queftion be repeated —Does not fuch an *exprefs agreement* clafh with our exprefs, as well as implied, obligations to France?

(3.) By enumerating, as contraband articles, in the treaty **with Great Britain**, certain articles which are declared free in the treaty **with France, *we may, confiftently with the latter, fupply Great Britain ; but, confiftently with the former, we cannot fupply France.***

Thus, *our treaty* with France (and, indeed, every treaty which we have) exprefsly declares, that, " in general, all provifions which ferve for the nourifhment of mankind and fuftenance of life ; furthermore, all kinds of cotton, hemp, flax, tar, pitch, ropes, cables, fail cloths, anchors and any part of anchors, alfo fhips, mafts, planks, boards and beams of what trees foever ; and all other things proper either for building, or repairing fhips, and all other goods whatever, which have not been worked into the form of any inftrument for war, by land or by fea, *fhall not be reputed contraband.*"

The treaty with Great Britain exprefsly declares, " that timber for fhip building, tar or rozin, copper in fheets, fails, hemp and cordage, and generally whatever may ferve directly to the equipment of veffels, unwrought iron, and fir planks only excepted, *fhall be objects of confifcation, whenever they are attempted to be carried to an enemy.*"

Whether this ftipulation can be confidered as founded on a principle of *reciprocity*, fince the articles declared to be contraband are *among our principal exports*, but *among the principal imports of Great Britain*, might have been adverted to, in tracing a former feature of the treaty ; but let it be now candidly anfwered, whether it is not *in collifion* with our previous engagements with France ? The right to make fuch a ftipulation, is not, at prefent, controverted ; but only the affertion, that *exercifing the right does not clafh in any degree* with the terms and fpirit of the French treaty. France exempts thofe important materials of our commerce from confifcation, in favour of all the world : Great Britain condemns them to confifcation, whenever they fhall be carried to her enemies ; and the compact is made, while France is one of her enemies !!

VI. *The Treaty with Great Britain is calculated to injure the United States, in the friendfhip and favour of other foreign nations.*

1. That the friendfhip and favour of France will be affected by the formation of fo heterogeneous an alliance with her moft implacable enemy, cannot be doubted, if we reafon upon any fcale applicable to the policy of nations, or the paffions of man. From that republic, therefore, if not an explicit renunciation of all connection with the United States, we may at leaft expect an alteration of conduct : and

finding the fuccefs which has flowed from the hoftile treatment that Great Britain has fhown towards us, fhe may be, at length, tempted to endeavour at *extorting from fear*, what fhe has not been able to obtain *from affection*. She will, probably, declare Great Britain in a ftate of blockade, for the purpofe of feizing our veffels in Europe; and fhe may inftitute courts for "legal adjudication," in order to confifcate our veffels in the Weft Indies. *Great Britain will then chuckle at the fcene.* No one can doubt that our embarrafments will gratify, not only the avowed objects, but the latent refentments, of that nation. Even if fhe could obliterate the memory of our revolution, fhe cannot, with pleafure, behold the fuccefsful experiment of a republican fyftem of government; nor the rapid advances of a commercial competitor. The moment fhe has produced a quarrel between America and France, fhe may exclaim, "*Delenda eft Carthago.*" America is again a colony! How different were the interefts and difpofitions of our tried friend! That our government fhould preferve its purity and independence—that our commerce and agriculture fhould attain their zenith—were views *once* congenial with the policy and affections of the French nation: Heart, head, and hand, fhe would have joined in promoting them, againft the arts and enmities of all the reft of the world! What a change, then, have we made!

"Look on *this* picture, and on *that*:
"The counterfeit prefentment of two *Allies!*
"Who would on this fair mountain leave to feed,
"To batten on that moor!"

2. During the war, we, likewife, formed a feafonable and ferviceable treaty with the United Netherlands; and, fhortly after the war, treaties were eftablifhed with Sweden, Pruffia, &c. But in order to avoid *even the appearance of clafhing or collifion* with the French treaty, the powers, thus early in courting our alliance, were not allowed thofe privileges of afylum for themfelves, and of excluding their enemies from our ports, which are conceded in the projected treaty to Great Britain. Have thofe nations no caufe for jealoufy **and** reproach? What principle of policy, or juftice, can vindicate the partiality and predilection, that has been thus fhown?

3. But the projected treaty (after an affected recognition of preexifting public treaties) declares, that while Great Britain and America continue in amity, no future treaty fhall be made, inconfiftent with the articles, that grant the high and dangerous privileges, that have been mentioned. Every nation of the earth (except France) is thus facrificed to the pride and intereft of Great Britain. And with what motive, or upon what confideration, is the facrifice made? It has been ftated in a former, and will be more fully fhewn in a future, feature of Mr. Jay's treaty, that the United States do not enjoy any equivalent for this, nor for any other, conceffion which is made to Great Britain: But the mifchief does not end with the folly of a lop-fided bargain. By granting thefe exclufive privileges to Great Britain, by declaring that no commercial favour

shall be conferred on other nations, without her participating in them, we have thrown away the surest means of purchasing, on any emergency, the good will and good offices of any other power: We cannot even improve the terms of our old treaty with France. For all the advantages of trade that Spain, Portugal, Holland, &c. might, and probably would, upon a liberal footing of reciprocity, have given us,—what have we now left, to offer as the basis of negociation and compact?

4. The alteration which the treaty makes in the relative situation of several nations with America, and the conduct, that is likely to be pursued by those nations, in order to counteract its effect, merit serious reflection. Will Spain see without some solicitude, the partition which we have made with Great Britain, of our territory on the eastern bank of the Mississippi? How would our projected treaty work, if France should recover Pondicherry, &c. in the East Indies; should subdue and retain the West India islands; should stipulate with Spain for the cession of Louisiana; and should conquer Nova Scotia? The curious *cordon* with which we have allowed Great Britain to circumvent us (and of which more will be said hereafter) being thus broken, how are we to calculate the consequences?

5. Considering the Indians as a foreign nation, is not the treaty calculated to exalt the character of Great Britain, and to depreciate the character of America, throughout the savage world? What right has Great Britain to negociate for Indians, within the limits of our jurisdiction? Suppose the existing western posts surrendered, may not Great Britain establish other posts in a contiguous or more advantageous station? Is she not left at liberty to pursue the fur trade in our territory as well as her own? Will not her enterprize in traffic, superior capital and experience, enable her to monopolize that trade? And will she not, in future, have the same motives, and the same means, to foment Indian hostilities, that have hitherto been indulged and employed, at the expense of so much American blood and treasure?

VII. *The Treaty with Great Britain is impolitic and pernicious, in respect to the domestic interests and happiness of the United States.*

1. If it is true, and incontrovertibly it is true, that the *interest* and *happiness* of America, consist (as our patriotic president, in his letter to Lord *Buchan*, declares) " in being little heard of in the great " world of politics; in having nothing to do in the political intrigues, " or the squabbles of European nations; but, on the contrary, in " exchanging commodities, and living in peace and amity with all the " inhabitants of the earth; and in doing justice to, and in receiving it " from, every power we are connected with;" it is is likewise manifest, that all the wisdom and energy of those who administer our government, should be constantly and sedulously employed to preserve, or to attain, for the United States, that enviable rank among nations. To *refrain from forming hasty and unequal alliances; to let*

commerce flow in its own natural channels; to afford every man, whether alien or citizen, a remedy for every wrong; and to refift, on the firft appearance, every violation of our national rights and independence, are the means beft adapted to the end which we contemplate. It maybe objected, that we are already involved in fome alliances, that have had a tendency rather to deftroy our public tranquillity, than to promote our public intereft. But a difference of circumftances will require and juftify a difference of conduct. For inftance—it was neceffary and politic, in the ftate of our affairs at the commencement of the revolution, to pay a premium for the friendfhip and alliance of France: we could not have infured fuccefs without the cooperation of that nation: and as *the price* that we paid for it was not greater than *the benefit* that we derived from it, we cannot now, with juftice, cavil at our bargain. But was the inducement *to* form an alliance with Great Britain, of a nature equally momentous? Is the advantage flowing from the facrifices that are made, equally compenfatory? Why fhould we, at this aufpicious feafon of our affairs, venture to undermine the fundamental maxim of our domeftic happinefs, *by wilfully obtruding on the great world of politics, or wantonly involving ourfelves in the political intrigues and the fquabbles of Europen nations?* Suppofe (as it is often alleged and fometimes proved) that our treaty with France is productive of inconveniences; will it happen in the political, any more than in the phyfical or moral world, that by multiplying the fources of evil, we fhall get rid of the evil itfelf? If, according to the *quondam* opinion of the friends of a Britifh alliance, our commerce has been reftrained in its operations; or if our government has been menaced in its peace and ftability, by a practical developement of *the terms* of our treaty with France, fhall we better our fituation, becaufe we make *another* treaty *upon the fame terms* with Great Britain; and furnifh *two* nations, inftead of *one*, with an opportunity to perplex and diftrefs us in purfuing our natural and laudable policy—*the policy of exchanging commodities, and living in peace and amity with all the inhabitants of the earth; doing juftice to, and in receiving it from, every power we are connected with!*

2. But even if the queftion was at large, and we were now *under a neceffity* of deciding, for the firft time, whether we would be allied to the monarchy of Great Britain, or to the republic of France, how would a rational eftimate of *the interefts and happinefs* of the United States (the true and only touch-ftone for folving, *in the mind of an American*, fuch an enquiry) lead us to decide? To *thofe members of the fenate*, who could regard *the twelfth article* of the treaty *as a mark of parental care and wifdom, by which Great Britain was fondly defirous of reftraining the exceffes of our commercial ardour; exceffes that might eventually and prematurely debilitate and deftroy us!* To *thofe members of the fenate*, who could, with filial gratitude, declare, *that an alliance with Great Britain was natural; that an alliance with France was artificial; fince, although we were partially indebted to France for our independence, we were entirely indebted to Great Britain for our being!* To all who can cherifh fuch ideas, or utter fuch language,

thefe ftrictures will be ungracious and unprofitable : but they claim a candid attention from *the patriot*, who remembers, that when *the parent* fought to deftroy, *the friend* interpofed to fave ; and from the *ftatefman*, who poffeffes too much wifdom to be influenced by prejudice, and too much fortitude to be controuled by fear.

Are the *interefts and happinefs* of the United States involved in the permanent eftablifhment of a republican government ? Yes :—Then fhe ought rather to cultivate the friendfhip of a republic, actuated by a fellow feeling, than the alliance of a monarchy impreffed with jealoufy and apprehenfion. Are *the intereft and happinefs* of the United States connected with her territorial and political independence? Yes : —Then fhe ought rather to fortify herfelf by an alliance with a nation, whofe territorial jurifdiction, and phyfical characteriftics, preclude the poffibility of collifion ; than attach herfelf to a nation whofe language, manners and habits, facilitate the execution of every attempt to encroach ; and whofe territorial poffeffions are in an irritating and dangerous contact with our own. Are *the intereft and happinefs* of America to be promoted by an active employment of the vaft ftore of *materials of the firft neceffity*, which nature has beftowed on her ; by the extenfion of her commerce ; and by the freedom of her navigation ? Yes :—Then fhe ought rather to court the countenance and protection of a nation, whofe occafions of envy are comparatively few ;—whofe temptations are to fofter, not to counteract, our fchemes of commercial opulence and enterprife ;—and whofe imperial glory and exiftence do not depend upon a claim of univerfal maritime fuperiority ;—rather than confent to bafk beneath the baneful fhade of an alliance with a nation, whofe very exiftence is, probably, the tremendous ftake in oppofition to our profperity : and whofe embraces, like the embraces of the tyrant's image, may be rendered the moft effectual inftruments of torture and deftruction. Are *the intereft and happinefs* of the United States dependant on the cordiality of their union, and the permanency of their government? And again—Do that cordiality and that permanency, depend upon the confidence and mutual good underftanding, which fubfift between the people who formed the government, and the officers whom the people have appointed to adminifter it ? Yes :—Then it would be the part of duty, as well as policy, in thofe officers to follow *the unanimous fentiment of the people*, by preferring a liberal and faithful alliance with France, to a conftrained and hypocritical alliance with Great Britain.

3. The firft ftriking effect of the treaty, *to endanger the interefts, and difturb the happinefs* of the United States, may be detected by a geographical fketch of the *cordon, or line of circumvallation, with which it enables Great Britain to fetter and enclofe us*. The proximity of Canada and the weftern pofts, has heretofore been a caufe of great uneafinefs ; but that is a trifling fource of vexation, compared with what we fhall have in future to encounter. Suppofe ten thoufand *radii* were drawn diverging from the centre of the United States ; not one of them could efcape the conventional circle of Britifh territory,

jurifdiction and occupancy.   Has an American occasion to travel to
the caſt or the north? *The barriers of Nova Scotia and Canada* prefent themſelves.   Is it his wiſh to penetrate the great weſtern wilder-
nefs? *A new ſet of Britiſh poſts* will intercept his progreſs, even if
he ſhall be allowed peaceably to paſs *the Britiſh colony* within the precincts and jurifdiction of Detroit.   Does buſineſs require him to croſs,
or float down, the Miſſiſſippi?   He may evade the vigilance of the
Spaniard, but he will find the eaſtern bank of the river monopolized
by Britiſh traders, and probably protected by Britiſh gun-boats.   He
is in hopes, however, to avoid all difficulty by a paſſage on the
ocean? Alas! our Atlantic harbours are crowded with prizes to
Britiſh privateers, and our ſea coaſt is lined with Britiſh cruiſers!
Yet, let us for a moment imagine, that this ill fated traveller has
ſurmounted his *domeſtic* obſtacles, whither can he fly, to be emanci-
pated from the *foreign* jurifdiction of Great Britain?   In the Weſt
Indies, his *cock boat* is meaſured and ſteered, according to the ſcale
and courſe preſcribed by the treaty.   In the Eaſt Indies he can hardly
exchange a commodity, or make a ſingle acquaintance, without the
Britiſh licenſe.   In Europe, if, during a Britiſh war, he carries
goods belonging to an enemy of Great Britain, they will be ſeized
as prize; if he takes ſhip-timber, tar, rozin, &c. they are liable to
be confiſcated as contraband; and if his cargo confiſts of proviſions,
the Britiſh may take it, *by treaty, at their own market price!*

One idea more about the boundary of the United States.   Before
the revolution, Great Britain had projected that general arrangement
and diviſion of her colonial poſſeſſions in America, which ſhe has
ſince, upon a ſmaller ſcale, carried into execution with reſpect to Canada.   The territory then intended to be allotted to the government
of the Canadas, was extended by a line running along the northern
boundaries of the eaſtern colonies, along the weſtern boundary of
Pennſylvania, and along the courſes of the Ohio, into the Miſſiſſippi.
Since we are left at a loſs for a poſitive definition of *the precincts and
jurifdiction of the weſtern poſts, as ceded by the treaty to the ſettlers under Britiſh titles*, may we not conjecture, that Great Britain contem-
plates the territorial extent of her original project?   Does not major
Campbell's unexpected pretenſion, and the conſtant claim of the Indians, *at the inſtigation of the Britiſh*, to eſtabliſh the Ohio as a boundary between them and the United States, give ſome countenance to
ſuch a conjecture?

4. But ſhould an American, not ſtimulated by the deſire of tra-
velling into foreign countries, be content to proſecute the objects of
his honeſt induſtry within the Britiſh territorial circle, bounding and
conſtituting *his own home*, will his condition be much better than the
condition of his itinerant fellow citizen?   What with the eſtabliſhment of Britiſh colonies and Britiſh ware-houſes; the naturalization
of Britiſh land-holders; and, in ſhort, the *unqualified admiſſion* of
Engliſhmen, owing allegiance to the Britiſh crown, throughout our
lakes, rivers and territory, while we are *excluded* from their ſea-ports,
company-lands, &c. &c. an American will hardly be able to find el-

bow-room for himself and family. Their pecuniary capital being larger; their means being easier; their experience being greater,— they must, inevitably, under such circumstances, become our merchants, manufacturers, farmers, &c. &c. They will import for us, *in their vessels*, all the products and fabrics of Europe, Asia and Africa —They will export for us, *in their vessels*, every article that our soil can furnish; our merchants will dwindle into clerks; our husbandmen will degenerate into the condition of the feudal villienage; and thus, in a short course of years, *America* **will** *probably exhibit the astonishing spectacle of a country possessed, cultivated, and* **enjoyed** *by aliens!* The ancient inhabitants of Great Britain, in a similar manner, invited those Saxons to their island as *friends and allies*, who soon afterwards became their *conquerors and masters.*

5. In such a state of things, *the interest and happiness* of the United States must languish and expire! At first the American mind will be corroded, by contrasting the elevation of *the guest* with the depression of *the host*. A struggle will probably ensue; but the influence of wealth, and the patronage of extensive commercial and manufactural institutions, &c. *will even divide the Americans themselves*; and, *by dividing*, capacitate the British settlers to rule them. Is this an idle phantom—a visionary suggestion? No! For, is not a great part of our trade, at this moment, monopolised by British subjects, under *the mask* of American citizenship? Has not the influence of British credits, and British politics already formed a considerable party in our government, and among our merchants? Disguise it as you will— let pride deny, and shame suppress the sentiment—still, it is too evident to every candid and discerning observer, that the only subsisting difference in the opinions and conduct of the citizens of America, arises from this fatal cause. Why, at the moment of reprobating *self-created societies for civil purposes*, do we gladly see the formation of *self-created societies for military purposes*; the city cohorts and Prætorian bands? Why are our merchants, who so anxiously called forth the voice of their fellow citizens in applauding the proclamation of neutrality, so circumspect and so torpid in giving their testimony about the treaty? How comes it, that amidst the acclamations of the 4th of July, the treaty is *toasted* in the little circle of English manufacturers, on the banks of the Passayik; and at the convivial tables of the English emigrants on the plains of the Génefee? How comes it that every man who prefers France to Great Britain—republicanism to monarchy,—is denominated *Antifederalist*, *Jacobin*, *Disorganiser*, *Miscreant*, &c. while men of another humour arrogantly and exclusively assume the titles of *Federalists*, *Friends to order*, &c. &c.? But let every honest American reflect seriously and seasonably, upon the means of promoting *the interest and happiness* of the United States, and he will disdain, as well as dread, to augment, by the adventitious force of treaties, that paramount interest, which Great Britain has already insidiously acquired in our commerce, navigation, manufactures, territory, and government.

6. Besides the injury eventually to be apprehended from these causes, the treaty is calculated to impair *the interest and happiness* of the United States, by producing an immediate and violent concussion in the federal atmosphere. For,

It ransacks the archives of our revolutionary transactions ; and re-judges the solemn judgments of our courts of justice.

It condemns individuals to the payment of debts, from which they had previously been discharged by law.

It makes the government of the union responsible for the contracts of private citizens, and the defalcations of bankrupts.

It disregards the freedom of our commerce and navigation : and it restrains the use of our staple commodities.

It does *not* exact a just indemnification for the detention of the western posts.

It does *not* require the payment, stipulated by the preceding treaty, *for the value* of the negroes carried off at the close of the war.

It does *not* provide for the freedom and safety of our seamen, in their intercourse with the British dominions.

Let any one of these propositions be separately analysed, and sufficient cause will be found to excite and justify popular dissatisfaction ; but view them combined, and the mind is shocked with an apprehension, that *the ratification of the treaty, may be the death-warrant of the union !*

VIII. *The British Treaty and the Constitution of the United States are at war with each other.*

1. Self-preservation is the first law of society, as well as of individuals : It is the radical principle of all political compacts. Nations (says *Vattel*) are bound to guard *their own preservation, and to pursue their own perfection.* We have incessant opportunities, indeed, of observing the operation of this universal rule ; in animals of *instinct*, as well as in animals of *reason* ; in the world of *things*, as well as in the world of *beings*.

2. Self-preservation, however, is a relative idea : it relates to the nature of the animal ; to the constitution of the society. A man may lose his *human character*, without destroying his *vital existence ;* and a government may be changed *in its essence*, without being subverted *in its forms*.

3. So, likewise, without open assault or positive violence, the sources of animal life may be poisoned, by the imperceptible contaminations of a luxurious habit : so, without the aid of terror or force, the legitimate foundations of government may be undermined, by the insidious encroachment of the rulers, and by the sedative acquiescence of the people. Governments, indeed, have too generally proved to be a kind of *political chrysalis*, passing, by progressive transmutations, from the grub of pure democracy, to the butterfly of absolute monarchy.

4. But it will not yet be denied in America, that as the people have the sole right to conflitute their government, the rule of *felf-preſervation* requires that the government ſhould be maintained, in practice as well as in theory, *ſuch as they have conſtituted it.* To render it, by any conſtruction of the written articles of our ſocial compact, *other than a republican government,* would be as fatal a ſubverſion, as daring uſurpation, or military conqueſt, could atchieve. For, what real difference does it make to a nation, whether its conſtitution is *ſeized upon* by an enterprizing individual, as in the Swediſh revolution of 1770 ; or *overthrown* by a triumphant warrior, as in the recent extinction of the Poliſh monarchy ; or *voted out of doors,* as in the diſorganizing edicts of the long parliament of England ? Thus, likewiſe, for one department of the government to aſſume the authority of another ; or, by conſtructive amplifications of its own juriſdiction, ſo to monopolize the attributes of government, as to render the other departments uſeleſs and inefficient, muſt ever be deemed an effectual ſubverſion of any conſtitution. The mode of diſtributing and organizing the powers of government, as well as the conſideration of the nature and extent of the powers to be delegated, eſſentially belongs to the people ; and in the body politic, as well as in the body natural, whenever any particular member abſorbs more than its allotted portion of the aliment, that is deſtined to vivify and invigorate the whole, debility and diſeaſe will infallibly enſue. After the emperors had uſurped the functions, privileges and powers of the ſenate, and of the popular magiſtrates of Rome, they preſerved the formalities of the commonwealth, but they trampled on the liberties of the people. Though the parliaments of France had long been deprived of every deliberative faculty, as the repreſentatives of the people, they were ſummoned to the laſt, as the miniſterial officers of the monarch, for the purpoſe of regiſtering his edicts.

5. The government of the United States, being then theoretically a *republican government,* and with great propriety denominated a *government of departments,* let us proceed to examine how far *the principles of ſelf-preſervation,* and the duty of *purſuing the perfection* of our political ſyſtem, are involved in the ratification of the projected treaty with Great Britain.

The ſecond ſection of the ſecond article of the conſtitution ſays, that, " The Preſident ſhall have power, by and with the advice and conſent of the ſenate, to make treaties, provided two-thirds of the ſenators preſent concur."

To the exerciſe of this power no immediate qualification, or reſtriction, is attached : but muſt we therefore ſuppoſe that the juriſdiction of the Preſident and ſenate, like the juriſdiction aſcribed to the Britiſh parliament, is omnipotent ? To place the authority of our Preſident and ſenate on the ſame footing with the prerogative of the king of Great Britain, will not be commenſurate with the objects to which the treaty extends. It muſt be remembered, that the treaty of peace, by which the rights of ſovereignty and ſoil were ceded by the king of Great Britain to the United States, was negociated and ratified under the pofitive fanction of an act of parliament : And it is exprefsly ftated in *Vattel*, that the king of Great Britain cannot, by *treaty*, confer the rights of citizenfhip on an alien. B. 1. c. 19. f. 214. Now, Mr. Jay's treaty does both thefe things (as will be hereafter demonftrated) without the intervention of the legiflative authority of the union.

6. The confequence of admitting this unqualified claim to omnipotence, in tranfacting the bufinefs of the nation, would be fo hoftile to the principle and prefervation of our government, that it is an indifpenfable duty *(obfta principiis)* to controvert and refift it. Whenever the Prefident and two-thirds of the Senate fhall be defirous to counteract the conduct of the houfe of reprefentatives ; whenever they may wifh to enforce a particular point of legiflation ; or whenever they fhall be difpofed to circumfcribe the power of a fucceeding Congrefs ; a treaty with a foreign nation, nay, a talk with a favage tribe, affords the ready and effectual inftrument for accomplifhing their views ; fince the treaty or the talk will conftitute the fupreme law of the land. That *fuch things may happen,* let the hiftory of Mr. Jay's miffion and negociation teftify.

7. If the extraordinary *treaty-making power* is paramount to the ordinary *legiflative power*—fupercedes its exercife—and embraces all its objects ; let us endeavour to trace whither the propofition will carry us.

The fifth article of the conftitution vefts a power in two-thirds of both houfes of Congrefs, to *propofe amendments to the conftitution.*

Let us fuppofe that a defect in our judiciary, or in any other department, operated injurioufly to a foreign nation,—could the Senate, and Prefident, uniting with that foreign nation, and excluding the houfe of reprefentatives *propofe an amendment upon the fubject ?* If they could by thefe means *originate,* might they not by other means *effectuate,* alterations in the fundamental points of our government ; and make, in fact, a new conftitution for us ?

By the eighth fection of the firft article, *Congrefs is* empowered to *borrow money* on the credit of the United States.

Suppofe it was deemed expedient to fubfidize Portugal, inftead of building frigates, to keep the Algerines within the ftreights of the Mediterranean :—Could two-thirds of the Senate and the Prefident, either borrow, or guarantee a loan for that purpofe *by treaty ?*

The fame fection empowers *Congrefs* to eftablifh uniform laws on *the fubject of bankruptcies.*

Suppofe Great Britain had remarked, that, as her fubjects were conftantly the creditors of the citizens of the United States, fhe was deeply interefted in our fyftem of bankrupt laws :—Had the Prefident and two-thirds of the Senate, a right to incorporate fuch a fyftem with the projected treaty ?

The fame fection empowers *Congrefs* to *coin money,* to regulate the value thereof, and of *foreign coin,* and fix the *ftandards of weights and meafures.*

Suppose the Birmingham manufacturers offered, on a cheap plan, to supply us with coin? Suppose Great Britain were pleased to insist upon our receiving her guineas at their English value, and upon our promising not to sweat, deface, or clip them, according to the current practice of the union? Suppose France were desirous that we should adopt the fanciful project of that republic, respecting weights and measures?—Could all, or any, of these propositions be acceded to and established *by treaty*?

The ninth section of the same article declares " that the migration or importation of such persons as the states now existing shall think proper to admit, shall not be prohibited by the Congress *prior* to the year eighteen hundred and eight."

Suppose Mr. Wilberforce had negociated on the part of Great Britain, instead of Lord Grenville, and had made the prohibition of the importation of slaves into the United States, in the year eighteen hundred and eight, *sine qua non:*—Could the President and two-thirds of the Senate admit and legitimise the stipulation *by treaty?*

By the constitution, *Congress* has the power to constitute tribunals inferior to the supreme court.

Suppose Great Britain desired, for the future, as well as for the past, to establish a tribunal of her own judges in America, for deciding controversies between British subjects and American citizens:—Could this be accomplished through the medium of a treaty?

By the constitution, *Congress* is endowed with the power of declaring war.

Suppose Lord Grenville had insisted, and Mr. Jay had approved, that the treaty should be an offensive and defensive alliance; and, that we should forthwith join Great Britain in her hostilities against France:—Could the President and Senate thus *negociate* us into a war?

By the constitution it is declared, " that no person holding any office, &c. under the United States, shall, without the consent of Congress, accept of any present, emolument, office or title, of any kind whatsoever, from any king, prince, or foreign state."

Suppose our envoy had been offered a present or a title by the British monarch—would the consent of the treaty be tantamount to the consent of Congress, for the purpose of approving and justifying his acceptance?

By the constitution it is provided, that all bills for raising revenues, shall originate in the house of representatives; and, that no money shall be drawn from the treasury, but in consequence of appropriations made by law.

Suppose Great Britain had stipulated, that as soon as the commissioners had fixed the sum due to her subjects for old debts, the President should draw a warrant for the amount, and that the same should be paid out of all public monies, in the treasury of the United States, prior to the payment of any antecedent appropriation by law:—Would this be the proper subject for a treaty, or for an impeachment?

E.

8. But fatigued and disgusted with displaying, thus hypothetically the monstrous consequences, which will inevitably flow from *the jurisdiction claimed on behalf of the President and Senate, to bind the United States by any treaty, and in all cases whatsoever;* let us particularly examine *the numerous and extravagant infractions* of the constitution, *which the projected treaty actually commits.* Recent as is the establishment of the federal constitution, it is, indeed, to be lamented, that the possibility of violating it, is not a matter of floating and fluctuating popular opinion; but a matter susceptible of fixed and positive proof. For, who does not recollect, that a bill touching the fundamental principle of the government (its representative quality) *after having passed both houses of Congress, was declared by the President to be unconstitutional; and, therefore, undeserving of his official approbation and signature?* Who can forget, that a law touching the essential properties of the judicial department of our government, *after being ratified by every organ of legislative authority* (the president, senate, and house of representatives) *was declared by chief justice Jay, and his associate judges, to be unconstitutional; and, therefore, incapable of being executed and enforced?* With such authoritative precedents (and there are many others that might be adduced from the transactions of individual states) of the possibility of deviating from the rule and meaning of our constitution, are we to be damned for political heresy, merely because we doubt, or deny *the infallibility of Mr. Jay's negociating talents?* And must every man be *accursed* (to use, for a moment, the intolerant language of the late secretary of the treasury, in his character of *the New York Camillus)* who thinks, that *the American envoy and the British minister were at least as likely to mistake, or misconstrue, the constitutional boundaries of the American government, as the president, senate, and house of representatives of the United States?* It is certainly, upon the whole, more candid, and more convincing, to put " the defence" of the treaty upon the *true trading ground,* taken by the New York, chamber of commerce;— to wit,—" *that we have made as good a market as such pedlers had a right to expect on the royal exchange; and that we cannot afford to fight, though we must submit to be plundered."*

9. Let us proceed, however, in examining the points on which *the British treaty is at war with the American constitution.*

(1.) *By the constitution of the United States, the* JUDICIAL POWER is vested in one supreme court, and in such inferior courts as *the Congress* may from time to time establish; and its jurisdiction embraces, among other things, " *controversies between a state, or citizens thereof, and foreign states, citizens or subjects."*

By the treaty, a tribunal other than the supreme court, or any inferior court established by Congress, is erected, with a jurisdiction to ascertain the amount of any losses or damages sustained " *by divers British* merchants and others, his majesty's subjects, *on account of debts,* &c. that still remain owing to them *by citizens or inhabitants* of the United States:" And it is agreed, " that in all such cases, where full compensation for such losses and damages cannot, *for whatever reason*, be actually had and received by the said creditors, in the ordinary course of justice, the United States will make full and complete compensation, for the same, to the creditors," &c.

Remarks. 1. It is the right of every independent nation to establish and maintain a judicial authority, co-extensive with its territorial possessions. The principle is indisputable, and it is incidentally recognized by Lord Mansfield and other great lawyers, in the celebrated controversy between the king of Prussia and Great Britain, relative to the Silesia Loan. 2. The constitutional tribunals of the United States were adequate to the administration of complete justice, in the very cases for which the treaty provides a special tribunal. 3. If it is possible in any case, with any nation, and at any time, to stipulate, *by treaty*, for the erection of a tribunal, in order to ascertain and liquidate debts due from citizens to foreigners, may it not be done in every case, with every nation, and at every time? 4. Is not the Court of Commissioners, in effect, an High Court of Errors and Appeals for the United States with power to revise and reverse every judgment, that has been given since the year 1783, *either in a federal or state court*, in every cause between a British subject and an American citizen? 5. Wherever the recovery of the principal debt has been protracted by *the forms of law*—wherever there has been *an abatement of interest*, by the compromise of the parties, or the verdict of a jury—wherever *the debtor has become insolvent*; this high court of Commissioners may sustain an appeal, and can award damages for the detention or loss of the debt. It is true, the treaty adds, that this " provision is to extend to such losses only as have been occasioned by *lawful impediments*;" but the *extent* of the discretion of the commissioners, in adjudging what constitutes a *lawful* impediment, is without limitation or controul; and the nature of the evidence, by which their minds are to be informed, is without rule or definition; since (in the language of the treaty) it may be " either according to the legal forms now respectively existing in the two countries, or in such other manner as the said commissioners shall see cause to require or allow." Thus, not only erecting a court unknown to our constitution, but admitting a species of proof, not recognized by the legal forms of our country. 6. Let us appeal to Mr. Jay himself, upon the constitutionality of such proceedings. By an act of Congress, the judges of the circuit courts were required to take, and report to the secretary at war, certain proofs in the case of invalids and pensioners. The judges refused (as we have already noticed) to execute the act, declaring it to be *unconstitutional*, as well on account of the nature of the duty imposed upon them, as on account of the revisionary power, which was vested in the secretary at war. *By the treaty*, the President and Senate will appoint commissioners, in conjunction with the king of Great Britain, to hold a court of appeals from every court in the union; and to determine judicial questions, upon private controversies, between British subjects and American citizens. Now, let us ask, whether it is more unconstitutional *for the legislature* to impose new and extraordinary duties upon a court, *exifting according to the conftitution*, than *for the executive* to create a new and extraordinary tribunal, *incompatible with the conftitution*; inafmuch as it can only act upon the alienation of the jurifdiction, *previoufly and exclufively* vefted in our domeftic courts;—the jurifdiction of hearing and deciding judicial queftions, upon private controverfies, between Britifh fubjects and American citizens? 7. But this is not the only infraction of the conftitution, involved in the arrangement alluded to—*the obligation of private contracts is transferred from individuals to the public.* The framers of the conftitution, in declaring that " all debts contracted, and engagements entered into, before its adoption, fhall be as valid againft the United States under the conftitution, as under the confederation," could hardly anticipate, that they charged the treafury of the union with the payment of all the outftanding debts of the individual citizens of America! And when Congrefs was vefted with a power " to lay and collect taxes, *to pay the debts*, and provide for the common defence and general welfare of the United States;" it certainly was never contemplated, that the government of America became the infurer of every Britifh merchant, againft litigious delays, and fraudulent or accidental bankruptcies! It cannot be fuggefted that Great Britain acts in a fimilar manner upon our complaints of the fpoliations on our trade. For, the injury that we have fuftained, originated *in an act of government*—the injured individuals are, in the *firft* inftance, bound to apply *to the Britifh courts of juftice*—and the public are only refponfible in the *laft* refort, for the individual aggreffors.

(2.) By the conftitution of the United States, Congrefs is empowered to eftablifh " an uniform rule of naturalization;" and that power has accordingly been exercifed in an act that provides, among other things, that ' no perfon heretofore profcribed by any ftate, fhall be admitted a citizen, except by an act of the legiflature of the ftate in which fuch perfon was profcribed."

By the Treaty, all the Britifh fettlers and traders, within the precincts or jurifdiction of the weftern pofts, are allowed an election either to remain Britifh fubjects, or to become citizens of the United States: And it is agreed, " that *Britifh fubjects* who now hold lands in the territories of the United States, may hold, grant, fell or devife the fame, to *whom they pleafe*, in like manner *as if they were natives;* and that neither they, *nor their heirs or affigns*, fhall, fo far as may refpect the faid lands, and the legal remedies incident thereto, be regarded *as aliens*."

Remarks. Is not the *treaty* at war with the *conftitution* in this great and delicate point of *naturalization?* A Britifh colony is, *ipfo facto*, by the magic of Mr. Jay's pen, converted into an American fettlement! Every *Britifh fubject*, who now holds lands (and when we recollect the recent fpeculations for the fale of lands, how can we calculate the extent of the adoption?) is, without ordeal or reftraint, endowed with all the rights of a *native American!* If it is poffible, by treaty, to give the rights of property to aliens, may not the *civil rights* of the community be difpofed of by the fame potent inftrument? If it is poffible, by treaty, to confer citizenfhip on the Britifh garrifon at Detroit, and its contiguous fettlers, why may we not, by treaty, alfo confer an inftantaneous citizenfhip on *every flight of emigrants*, that fhall haften to our fhores from Germany or Ireland? It may not be amifs here to intimate a doubt of *the power* of the federal government to regulate the tenure of real eftates : it is no where exprefsly given, and, therefore, cannot be conftitutionally implied ; and it feems to be among the neceffary and natural objeēts of ftate legiflation. But let us prefume (**what is** highly probable) that there are amongft the fettlers within the precinēts or jurifdiēlion of the weftern pofts, certain *proſcribed perſons*—can the treaty, in fpite of *the law*, reftore them to the rights of citizenfhip, without the authoritative affent of the ftate that profcribed them? Again—Is every man whofe eftate was liable to confifcation as a traitor, or as an alien, in confequence of the revolution, entitled *now to hold lands as a native?* The Fairfax claim in Virginia ; the claim of the Penns in Pennfylvania ; and the claims of Galloway, Allen, &c. &c. may hence derive a dangerous principle of refufcitation. *Look to it well.*

(3.) By the conftitution, Congrefs is empowered to regulate commerce with foreign nations.

By the treaty, the commerce of the United States, not only directly with Great Britain, but incidentally with *every* foreign nation, is regulated.

Remarks. There is not a fource of *legiflative jurifdiēion*, upon the fubjeēt of commerce, which is not abforbed by this *executive compaēt.* The power of regulating commerce with foreign nations, is exprefsly and fpecifically given *to Congrefs :* Can a power fo given to one department, be divefted by implication, in order to amplify and invigorate another power, given in general terms to another department? But more of that hereafter.

(4.) By the conftitution, Congrefs is empowered to regulate commerce with the Indian tribes.

By the treaty, it is agreed, that " it fhall at all times be free to Britifh fubjeēts, &c. and alfo to the Indians dwelling on either fide of the boundary line of the United States, freely to pafs and repafs by land or inland navigation, into the refpeēive territories and countries of the two parties on the continent of America, &c. and freely to carry on trade and commerce with each other." The treaty, likewife, provides, that " no duty of entry fhall ever be levied by either party *on pelt ies* brought by land, or inland navigation into the faid territories refpeēively ; nor fhall the Indians paffing or repaffing with their own proper goods and effeēts, of whatever nature, pay for the fame any impoft or duty whatever."

Remarks. It is eafy to perceive that the ftipulations, in favour of the Indians, were introduced at the inftance of Great Britain ; and her motives are not even attempted to be difguifed. Her traders will boaft of the favour and fecurity, which fhe has compelled America to grant to the Indians ; and fo engage their confidence and attachment ; while the privilege of free paffage and the exemption from duties,

will inevitably throw the whole fur-trade into the hands of the British.
The furrender of the western posts, under such circumstances, can
produce no loss to Great Britain, and will certainly be of no advantage to America: It will not add a shilling to the profits of our Indian
traffic ; nor infure us a moment's fufpenfion of Indian hostilities ! **But,**
to profecute our *constitutional* enquiry—what right is there, by *treaty*,
to regulate our commerce with the Indian tribes ? Whenever a treaty
of peace and amity has *heretofore* been concluded with the Indians, it
has been the constitutional practice of the President, to call on Congrefs to regulate the commerce with them.   Such calls were totally
unneceffary, if the same thing might as well and as lawfully be done
by treaty ; and if it could not be done by treaty in the cafe of the *Indians,* neither could it be done by treaty in the cafe of a *foreign nation :* For, both are expreffed in the *fame terms,* and included in the
fame member of the fection.   " Congrefs fhall have power (fays the
constitution) to regulate commerce with foreign nations, and among
the feveral states, and with the Indian tribes."   What right is there
by *treaty* to declare that *no duty* of entry fhall ever be levied by either
party *on peltries, &c.* (and a fimilar promife is made in cafes that
more immediately affect Great Britain) fince *Congrefs* has the fole
power to lay and collect taxes, *duties,* &c. to pay the debts, and provide for the common defence, and general welfare of the United
States ? If we may, *negatively,* fay, *by treaty,* that certain duties fhall
not be laid, may we not *affirmatively* fay, *by treaty,* that certain other duties fhall be laid ? And then what becomes of that part of our conftitution, which declares, " that all bills for raifing revenue fhall originate in the houfe of reprefentatives ?" But let us imagine for a moment, that it is in the power of the Prefident and Senate to regulate
our commerce with the Indian tribes ; *ought not the regulation to be
made with the Indians themfelves ?* Why fuffer Great Britain to negociate and ftipulate for Indians actually refiding within the territory
of the United States ? Is fuch a conceffion confiftent with the dignity
and independence of our government—with the peace and intereft of
the nation ? Let Mr. Randolph's letter to Mr. Hammond, on the
conduct of general Simcoe and major Campbell be referred to, as an
anfwer to this queftion.   It is not, at prefent, **within reach to be**
quoted ; but its contents were too important to have already efcaped
the memory of any reflecting American.

   (5.) By the conftitution, Congrefs is empowered " to define and
punifh piracies and felonies committed on the high feas, and offences
againft the law of nations."

   By the treaty, the definition and punifhment of certain offences,
not known by any law of the union, is declared and permitted ; to
wit—1ft. For accepting commiffions or inftructions from any foreign
prince or ftate, to act againft Great Britain.   2d. For accepting any
foreign commiffion or letter of marque for arming any privateer, &c.
Great Britain may punifh an American citizen *as a pirate.*   3d. For
not treating Britifh officers *with that refpect which is due to the commiffions they bear,* and for offering any infult to fuch officers, the of-

fenders shall be punished *as disturbers of the peace and* amity *between America and Great Britain.* 4th. For making a prize upon the subjects of Great Britain, the people of every other belligerent nation (except France) shall be punished *by a denial of shelter or refuge, in our ports.*

Remarks. To define crimes, and apportion punishments, is the **peculiar** province of the *legislative authority* of every free government: **but it is** obvious, from the foregoing recapitulation, that the *executive authority* has likewise encroached upon that province, by the instrumentality **of** its *treaty-making* power. Can a citizen be surrendered *by treaty* to all the pains and penalties of *piracy?* Then *by treaty,* he might be subjected to all the pains and penalties of *treason.* It is true, **that the** constitution reserves to itself *the exclusive right* of declaring what shall constitute *treason;* but it is equally true, that it bestows on Congress the *exclusive right* to define and punish *piracy:* and the invasion of *the right to define* in one case, is as unconstitutional as the invasion of *an actual definition* in the other. But what legitimate authority can *a treaty* suggest, in order to justify the restraint upon that right of expatriation, which Congress itself has not ventured to restrain, while legislating on subjects of a similar class? It is not intended to convey the slightest doubt of the power and propriety of controuling our citizens in their conduct towards *foreign nations,* while they are within the reach of *domestic coercion:* but to prohibit an American freeman from going whither he pleases, in quest of fortune and happiness——to restrict him from exercising, *in a foreign country, and in a foreign service,* his genius, talents and industry; to denounce him for seeking honour, emolument or instruction, by enlisting *within the territory, and under the banners* of another nation——to do such things, is to condemn the principle of our own **policy,** by which we invite all the world to fill up the population of **our country:** To do such things is, in fact, to prostrate the boasted **rights of man.** It is hardly worth a pause to ask, What proportion of **respect** is due to the commission of a British officer? and what degree of punishment the refusal or neglect to pay it, may deserve?

(6.) By the constitution it is declared, that " no tax or duty shall be laid *on articles exported from any state.*"

By the treaty, " it is expressly agreed and declared that the United States will prohibit and restrain the carrying any melasses, sugar, coffee, cocoa, or cotton, in American vessels, either from his majesty's islands, *or from the United States,* to any part of the world."

Remarks. This is an extract, it is true, from the twelfth article of the treaty; but it equally serves to show the probability of attempts to violate the constitution. Besides, the advocates for the treaty are hasty and premature, when they desire to throw the twelfth article entirely out of consideration: for, by that proposition, *though they should save the treaty, they effectually destroy its author.* They are hasty and premature for another reason: the twelfth article is to be *suspended for the declared purpose of negociating something as a substitute;* and, therefore we must consider its principle, in order to ascertain how far *any modification* of it could be rendered palatable. But, *on constitutional ground,* when it is declared, that *no duty* shall *by law* be laid on articles exported from any state, is it not absurd, or wicked to suppose, that *by treaty* the exportation of *the articles themselves* can be prohibited? The obvious intention of *the constitution* is ·to encourage *our export trade ;*—the immediate effect of *the treaty* is to obstruct and annihilate it.

(7.) There are many other points in which *a collision occurs between the constitution and the treaty,* but to which the scope and nature of these strictures will not admit a full attention. It may be cursorily remarked, however, that a *cession of territory,* which will, probably, be the consequence of *settling anew the boundaries* of the United States, and even the actual cession of the precincts of the western posts, *though in favour of individuals,* are subjects for serious reflection. If a part of the United States may be ceded—if a whole state may be ceded, what becomes of the guarantee of a republican form of government to every state? The propriety of presenting this consideration to the public mind, will be allowed by those who know, that, *in the course of the senatorial debate, the* right *of* ceding by treaty *a whole state, nay,* any number *of the states, short of a majority, was* boldly asserted, *and* strenuously argued ! ! !

(8.) It may not be amiss, likewise, to add, that our government has no more right to *alienate powers that are given,* than it has to *usurp powers that are not given.* For instance, *an act of Congress* could not (and can a treaty ?) surrender the right of sequestering the property of a hostile nation—the right of giving commercial preferences to a friendly nation—and the right of suspending a ruinous intercourse with any nation? Great clamours have been raised against *the exercise* of these rights ; and, undoubtedly, they should only be used *in the last resort ;* but they are rights *recognised by the law of nations ;* and they are rights often essential to the duties of *self-preservation,* and sometimes necessary to the accomplishment of *reciprocal justice.*

10. Having taken this *review of the actual warfare between the constitution and Mr. Jay's diplomatic work,* and of the destructive consequences of the claim of *the executive, to bind the United States, in all cases whatsoever, by treaty ;* let us recur to the position with which the present feature was introduced, namely, *the duty of preserving the constitution, such as it was made and intended by the people,* and we shall find, by a faithful comparison of theory with practice, that *the government of the United States may be transformed through the medium of the treaty-making power, from a republic to an oligarchy— from a free government of several departments,* legislative, judicial and executive—*to the simple aristocratical* government of a President and Senate.

11. This fatal effect, however, of converting our government from the system which the people *love,* to a system which they *abhor,*— from what it was made in theory, to what it was never intended to be made by practice—can only proceed from *error* or *corruption.* It

would ill become the writer of these strictures, who so freely, but it is hoped, so fairly, expresses an opinion, to impute to any man or set of men, a sinister and traiterous design against the constitution of our common country. The denunciations fulminated by *the New-York Camillus*, and his small circle of coadjutors, harmlessly expand themselves in the violence of their explosion : like the denunciations of *the Tiara*, they spring from *an arrogant claim of infallibility ;* and like them too, will only excite *the derision or the disgust of an enlightened nation*. Is it credible, that every citizen of the United States, from Georgia to New-Hampshire, who reprobates Mr. Jay's treaty, must either be *an enemy to our government*, or *a rancorous incendiary ?* Is it to be presumed that no man can utter a sentence of disapprobation respecting *the principles* of the treaty, without feeling a sentiment of animosity, respecting *the person* of the negociator ? Are we really such slaves to faction ;—so trammelled with party ;—so insensible to virtue, truth and patriotism ;—that every thought which we conceive, every expression which we use, on this momentous occasion, must be connected with the possible (but it is ardently hoped the distant) event *of electing a successor to the present chief magistrate of the union?* Yet, such are the base and sordid motives, passionately and wantonly ascribed by *Camillus* and the scanty troop of advocates, who follow him *in supporting the treaty, to the great host of the American people, rising* (as it were) *in mass to condemn it.*

If it could be thought a convenient, a reputable, or a necessary task, how successfully might *the argument of recrimination* be employed! Who, it could be asked, are *the persons* that support the treaty ? What are *the motives* that actuate them ? Is it surprising that *the men who advised* the treaty, or that the THE MAN *who composed it*, should endeavour, by the force of ingenuity, art, or defamation, to rescue it from general malediction and impending ruin? Was it not to be expected, that a *faction, uniformly eager to establish an alliance with Great Britain, at the expence of France,* would strenuously attempt to procure the ratification of *any instrument*, calculated to accomplish that object? Does not consistency require from *him, who openly projected in the Federal Convention*, and from those, *who secretly desire in the execution of public offices*, the establishment of an aristocracy, under the insidious title of *an energetic scheme of government*, that they should approve and countenance every practical application of *any medium*, by which the barriers that separate our constitutional departments, may be overthrown, and the occasions for interposing the popular sanction of the legislature, may be superceded or avoided ? Is it not *natural*, that British merchants and British agents—is it not *necessary*, that British debtors and British factors,—should clamorously unite, or tacitly acquiesce, in the applause bestowed upon a compact, which, however detrimental to America, is beneficial to Great Britain—the nation of chief importance to the allegiance and affections of some of those characters, and to the opulence and subsistence of all ? Or, if the paltry idea of an *electioneering* plan must be forced upon our consideration, is it not, at least, as likely, that *the party, which aims at making a Prefident of Mr. Jay, will, on that ground alone, exert it-self in* " The Defence" *of the treaty,* as that the party, which is defirous of conferring the fame elevated office on Mr. Jefferfon, will, for no other reafon, attempt to blaft the fruits of his competitor's negociation? Confidering, indeed, that *Camillus* himfelf, by con-fining his "Defence" *to the treaty as advifed to be ratified by the fe-nate,* virtually abandons the treaty as negociated and concluded by *Mr. Jay:*—and alfo, confidering that a part of *Camillus's* defence of the *prefent treaty* arifes from the *ambiguity* that Mr. Jay had left in the *former treaty* with Great Britain (upon which, however, his character as a negociator was founded) we might be led to fuppofe, that Mr. Jay's pretenfions to the wifdom of a ftatefman, and to the ftation of a Prefident, were not deemed, *even by his own party,* to be any longer tenable; but that *Camillus* ftill cordefcends, on the obvious prefumption of a fubfifting rivalfhip, to impeach the minifte-rial character, and to depreciate the official performances, of Mr. Jefferfon.

But why fhould we arbitrarily *abufe,* inftead of endeavouring ra-tionally to *convince* each other? We all have the fame right, from natural and from focial law, *to think and to fpeak :* it is true, that we do not all poffefs the fame powers of reafon, nor the fame charms of eloquence; but when men are on *an equality in the poffeffion,* as well as in *the right of exercifing,* thofe endowments, there can be no ami-cable way of adjufting a difference of opinion, but that which is adopted for adjufting all the other differences of a free people—*an appeal to the voice of the majority!* Now, let it be allowed (and fo far ought it to be allowed, but no farther) that Mr. Jay; who negociated the treaty; the twenty members of the fenate, who affented to a con-ditional ratification; and Mr. Hamilton, and the New-York cham-ber of commerce, who have appeared in fupport of it (an enumera-tion that comprifes, it is believed, all that have hitherto *avowed a perfect approbation*) are in the poffeffion of as great a proportion of information, integrity and talents, as *a like number* of citizens, fe-lected for their approved wifdom, virtue and patriotifm, from the aggregate of thofe who have publicly condemned the treaty; and then let it be candidly anfwered, which fcale in the balance muft, of right, preponderate? After fuch a felection, there will ftill remain the great body of the community in oppofition to a ratification; and, as members of that community, thoufands of individuals, who hon-ourably ferved during the late war, in the field and the cabinet, and many of whom at this moment ferve with zeal, fidelity and wifdom in the various departments of government. Is it not then the fymp-tom of an arrogant vanity—of a tyrannical difpofition—to ftigmatife fuch an oppofition to *a projected meafure,* with the name of ' *Faction ?*' The violence offered to Mr. Hamilton's perfon in New-York, and to Mr. Bingham's houfe in Philadelphia, have juftly excited the in-dignation of every fincere republican; but even that reprehenfible and odious conduct is not to be compared to the enormous guilt of endeavouring to *force* the opinion of a *few* individuals upon *the people,* as the ultimate teft of political truth; and to caft an *odium* upon the late conventions, in which (according to the language of the conftitution) "the people were peaceably affembled, to petition the government for the redrefs (or rather the prevention) of a grievance."

But let the pardon of the reader be granted for *this digreffion*; and we will return to a delineation of the feature that lies before us.

12. Declining, then, either to create, or to follow, a bad example, let us afcribe the deviation from the principles of our conftitution to an *erroneous conftruction*, rather than to *a wilful perverfion*; and let us exert our fkill in averting the evil that threatens, rather than indulge our refentment in convicting thofe who labour to produce it.

Our government, therefore, being *a government of departments*, it is (as we have already obferved) inconfiftent with *the duty of felf-prefervation*; or, in other words, it muft proceed from an error in *conftruction*; that *one* department fhall affume and exercife all, or any, of the powers, of all, or any, of the other departments.— "The departments of government (to adopt the elegant figure ufed by an excellent judge, in a late admirable charge to a Philadelphia jury) are planets that revolve, each in its appropriate orbit, round the conftitution, as the fun of our political fyftem." Thus, if the legiflative, executive, or judicial departments fhall encroach, one upon the orbit of the other, the deftruction of the order, ufe, and beauty of the political fyftem, muft as inevitably enfue, as the deftruction of the order, ufe, and beauty of the planetary fyftem would follow, from a fubverfion of the effential principles of attraction, repulfion and gravity.

13. It was neceffary, however, that the power of making treaties with foreign nations, fhould be vefted in one of the departments of the government: but the power of making treaties is not, in its nature, paramount to every other power; nor does the exercife of that power naturally demand an exclufive jurifdiction. A nation may carry on its *external commerce* without the aid of *the treaty-making power*; but it cannot manage its *domeftic concerns* without the aid of the *legiflative power*: the legiflative power is, confequently, of fuperior importance and rank to the treaty-making power. Again: *The legiflative power exercifed conformably to the conftitution*, muft be direct, univerfal, and conclufive in its operation and force upon the people; but *the treaty-making power* is fcarcely in any inftance independent of legiflative aid to effectuate its efforts, and to render its compacts obligatory on the nation. A memorable occurrence in the Englifh hiftory will ferve to illuftrate both of thefe pofitions: It is the fate of *the commercial part of the famous treaty of Utrecht*, concluded between France and England in the year 1712. "The peace (fays Ruffel in his Hiftory of Modern Europe, vol. 4. p. 457) was generally difliked by the people, and all impartial men reprobated the treaty of commerce with France, as foon as the terms were known. Exception was particularly taken againft the 8th and 9th articles, importing "That Great Britain and France fhould mutually

enjoy all the privileges in trading with each other, which either granted to the most favoured nation ; that all prohibitions should be removed, and no higher duties imposed on the French commodities, than on those of any other people." The ruinous tendency of these articles was perceived by the whole trading part of the kingdom. It was accordingly urged, when a bill was brought into the house of commons for confirming them, that the trade with Portugal, the most beneficial of any, would be lost, should the duties on French and Portuguese wines be made equal, &c. &c. These and similar arguments induced the more moderate tories to join the whigs, *and the bill was rejected by a majority of nine votes.* In relating the same transaction, Smollet's history of England, vol. 2. p. 242, 246, contains some passages too remarkable to be omitted on the present occasion. " Against the 8th and 9th articles, (says the historian) the Portuguese minister presented a memorial, declaring, that should the duties on French wines be lowered to the same level with those that were laid on the wines of Portugal, his master would renew the prohibition of the woolen manufactures, and other products of Great Britain. Indeed, all the trading part of the nation exclaimed against the treaty of commerce, which seems to have been concluded in a hurry, before the ministers fully understood the nature of the subject. This precipitation was owing to the fears that their endeavours after peace would miscarry, from the intrigues of the whig faction, and the obstinate opposition of the confederates." " Another bill (continues the same writer, in a subsequent page) being brought into the house of commons, for rendering the treaty of commerce effectual, *such a number of petitions were delivered against it,* and so many solid arguments advanced by the merchants, who were examined on the subject, that even a great number of tory members were convinced of the bad consequence it would produce to trade, and voted against the minister on this occasion."

Perhaps there cannot, in the annals of all the nations of the earth, be found two cases more parallel than the one which is thus recorded in the English history, and the one which at present agitates the American nation.—1. All impartial men reprobated both treaties, as soon as the terms were known. 2. The admission of the opposite contracting party to an unqualified participation in trade, with the most favoured nation, is, in both cases, a principal source of complaint. 3. The removal of all prohibitions, and the surrender of the right to impose higher duties on the commodities of the opposite contracting party, than on those of any other people, are, in both cases, condemned. 4. The good and the intelligent, of all parties, have united their influence, in both cases, to prevent a confirmation of articles of so ruinous a tendency. 5. The whole nation, in both cases, have exclaimed against the treaty. 6. Both treaties were concluded in a hurry, before the ministers fully understood the nature of the subject. 7. Innumerable petitions (and who will NOW deny the propriety of exercising the American right to petition ?) were delivered against both treaties. 8. And the Portuguese minister declared, in effect, of the treaty of Utrecht (*mutatis mutandis*) what the minister of France will, probably declare of the treaty of London (but what America surrenders the right of saying at any time to Great Britain) " If you ratify your alliance with the British, you must surrender your alliance with France." If such a wonderful similarity of circumstances concur *in the negociation, terms, and reception* of these memorable instruments, let us hope that the guardian angel of American liberty and prosperity, has, also, doomed them finally to experience a *merited similarity of fate!*

14. But having thus shown, that, *even in Great Britain,* the treaty-making prerogative is *neither paramount nor exclusive* (though *the generality* of judge Blackstone's expressions on the subject, would, perhaps, lead to that preposterous conclusion) we might be satisfied to presume, on general principles, that so high a claim of jurisdiction could not be maintained, at least, on the part of our president and senate. Yet, let us endeavour, by the infallible test of the constitution, to put the matter, if possible, beyond doubt and controversy; and, having established that each department of the government should be confined to its proper orbit, let us endeavour to ascertain, what that orbit is, in relation to the *treaty-making power.*

(1.) The power of the president and senate to make treaties, is given, (as we have already stated) *in general and unrestricted terms.*

But the powers given to Congress (except in an instance to be hereafter noticed) *are definite in their terms, and appropriated in their objects.*

Let us ask, then, by what rule of construction a power *primarily and specifically* given to one body, can be assumed and exercised by another, to which, *in a subsequent clause,* a mere *general* authority is given?

Upon the common law principles of construction, *the specific powers* would clearly, in such a case, be deemed a reservation and exception out of *the general grant.* But even according to a rule furnished by the constitution itself, the same result will be produced. Thus, the twelfth ratified amendment declares, " that the powers not delegated to the United States by the constitution, are reserved to the states respectively, or to the people." Now, if the general power granted for the purpose of making treaties, can set at nought the jurisdiction specifically given to Congress for the purpose of making laws, may it not, with equal propriety and effect, overleap the boundary thus interposed between popular rights and constituted powers? In the one case, the reservation is expressly declared—in the other, it is necessarily implied.

(2. But if the delegation of a *general power* does, *ipso facto,* convey a right to embrace, in the exercise of that power, every authority not incompatible with its objects, the consequence will be, that *Congress may enter into treaties as well as the president and senate.*

For, Congress is vested with a jurisdiction " to make all laws, which shall be necessary and proper for carrying into execution their own powers:" and what laws are, in that respect, necessary and proper, they must, from the nature of the thing, be the judge.

Suppose, therefore, that Congress was desirous of forming *an alliance, offensive and defensive, with France,* but could not obtain the constitutional number of two-thirds of the senate for accomplishing the measure *by treaty,—an act of Congress, in order to regulate commerce with that nation,* would afford as effectual a mode (according to the new doctrine) since the act, on the pretext of an equivalent for commercial advantages, might *legislate* us into the coveted alliance. The temptation and facility of proceeding in this way is obvious ;—the passing of a law requiring but a majority of the senate ; whereas the ratification of a treaty requires the concurrence of two-thirds of the members of that body.

(3.) It is not, however, necessary to mingle and confuse the departments of our government, contrary to the first principles of a free republic ; nor to make *a part* of our political system *equal to the whole,* contrary to the soundest axioms of demonstrative philosophy, in order to give a just, efficient and salutary effect to the treaty-making power of the president and senate.   For although,

In the *first* place, the *treaty-making* power cannot bind the nation by *a decision* upon any of the subjects, which the constitution expressly devolves upon the *legislative power :*

Yet, in the *second* place, the treaty-making power may *negociate conditionally,* respecting the subjects that constitutionally belong to *the decision of the legislative power ;*

And, in the *third* place, *every other subject,* proper for the national compact of a republic, may be *negociated and absolutely concluded by the treaty-making power.*

(4.) That such a distinction was intended by the framers of our present excellent constitution, the reasons that have been glanced at, must, it is thought, sufficiently prove to every ingenuous mind : But let one argument more be adduced.

By the ninth article of the old confederation, it was declared, " That the United States, in Congress assembled, shall have *the sole and exclusive right and power of determining on peace and war.*"

By the existing constitution of the United States, it is provided, " That Congress shall have power *to declare war,* grant letters of marque and reprisal," &c.

Now, it is evident, that by omitting to deposit *with Congress* the power of *making peace,* in addition to the power of *declaring war,* the framers of our present government, had in full view the division of its department, and the corresponding distribution of its powers.

Congress, *under the confederation* was a *single* body, and therefore, necessarily possessed of all the little legislative, executive, and judicial authority, which *the states* had been pleased to delegate *to the union.*

The government of the United States, on the contrary, is a compound system, of which the Congress is only *the legislative department :* and, therefore, the executive and judicial functions are elsewhere to be sought for and exercised.

Hence it is, that although the power of *declaring war is* (as it ought to be) *left with Congress*, the power of *making peace is* (as it ought to be) *transferred to the executive;* being a natural appendage of the general power of *making treaties.*

This deduction serves likewise to demonstrate, that the framers of the constitution, did not intend to leave the powers that are *specifically* given to Congress, at the mercy of the power that is *generally* given to the president and senate. By expressing a positive jurisdiction in favour of the former, it excludes a claim of jurisdiction in favour of the latter.

(5.) Nor is it in *the power of making treaties only*, that the constitution has abridged *the executive department* of its customary attributes, in order to augment the sources of *legislative jurisdiction.*

In Great Britain (for instance) *the executive* possesses the power of making peace ; of granting letters of marque and reprisal ; of regulating weights and measures ; of coining money, regulating the value thereof, and of foreign coins ; of erecting courts of judicature ; of conferring the rights of denizenship on aliens, &c. &c.

In the United States the power for all those purposes is absolutely vested *in the legislature.*

15. On reviewing the various positions that have been taken in the course of these strictures, a desire is felt to exhibit the corroborative opinions of men who have been justly valued by the public : It will be useful to the reader, as well as pleasing to the writer, to indulge the disposition in a few instances, and in a brief manner.

(1.) It has been said, that *the power of regulating commerce belonged to Congress.*

The report of Mr. Mason (a member of the federal convention) on that subject, was delivered in the convention of Virginia as follows : "With respect to commerce and navigation, I will give you, to the best of my information, the history of that affair. This business was discussed [in the convention] at Philadelphia for four months ; during which time the subject of commerce and navigation was often under consideration ; and, I assert, that eight out of twelve, for more than three months, voted for requiring two-thirds of the members present in each house to pass commercial and navigation laws. True it is, that afterwards it was carried by a majority as it stands. If I am right, there was a great majority for two-thirds of the states in this business, till a compromise took place between the northern and southern states ; the northern states agreeing to the temporary importation of slaves ; and the southern states conceding, in return, that navigation and commercial laws should be on the footing in which they now stand."

(2.) It has been said, that *the treaty-making power could not cede a part of the union, nor surrender a citizen to be punished as a pirate.*

The opinion of Mr. Randolph (a member of the federal convention, and now secretary of state) delivered in the same convention, contains the following passage : "I conceive, that neither the life, nor the property of any citizen, nor the particular right of any state, can be effected by a treaty."

Mr. Madison, also, justifying and recommending the adoption of the constitution to his fellow citizens, says, with respect to *the treaty-making power*—" I am persuaded, that when this power comes to be thoroughly and candidly viewed, it will be found right and proper. Does it follow, because this power is given to Congress, that it is absolute and unlimited ?—I do not conceive that power is given to the president and senate to dismember the empire, or to alienate any great, essential right. I do not think the whole legislative authority have this power. The exercise of the power must be consistent with the object of the delegation."

(3.) It has been said, *the right of suspending a commercial intercourse with any nation, and the right of sequestering an enemy's property, &c. were rights essential to an independent government, and recognised by the law of nations.*

Vattel contains the following, among many other passages on those subjects :

" Every state has a right to prohibit the entrance of foreign merchandise, and the people who are interested have no right to complain of it, as if they had been refused an office of humanity." B. 1. c. 8. s. 90.

" It depends on the will of any nation to carry on commerce with another, or to let it alone." Ibid. s. 92.

" The goods even of the individuals in their totality ought to be considered as the goods of the nation, in regard to other states. From an immediate consequence of this principle, if one nation has a right to any part of the goods of another, it has a right indifferently to the goods of the citizens of that part, till the discharge of the obligation." Ibid. s. 81, 82.

" It is not always necessary to have recourse to arms, in order to punish a nation : the offended may take from it, by way of punishment, the privileges it enjoys in his dominions ; seize, if he has an opportunity, on some of the things that belong to it, and detain them till it has given him a just satisfaction." B. 2. c. 18. s. 340.

" When a sovereign is not satisfied with the manner in which his subjects are treated by the laws and customs of another nation, he is at liberty to declare, that he will treat the subjects of that nation in the same manner that his are treated." Ibid. s. 341.

(4.) It has been said that the constitution ought to be preserved *such as the people have made it* ; that, of course, the departments of government ought to be kept separate and distinct, *each revolving in its proper orbit*, and that *no other judicial tribunal* could be erected by *a law of the legislative power*, much less by *a treaty of the executive power*, than *what the constitution prescribes, or expressly permits.*

On this interesting subject we fortunately possess the opinions of the judges of the supreme court, and of the judges of some of the district courts, in the case of the act of Congress (already more than once alluded to) *which they have unanimously adjudged to be uncon-stitutional and void.*

Extract from the opinion of *judges* IREDELL and SITGREAVES.

"*First :* That the legislative, executive and judicial departments are each formed in a separate and independent manner ; and that the ultimate basis of each is the constitution only ; within the limits of which each department can alone justify any act of authority.

"*Secondly :* That the legislature, among other important powers, unquestionably possesses that of establishing courts, in such a manner as to their wisdom shall appear best, limited by the terms of the constitution only ; and to whatever extent that power may be exercised, or however severe the duty they may think proper to require, the judges, when appointed in virtue of any such establishment, owe implicit and unreserved obedience to it.

"*Thirdly :* That at the same time such courts cannot be warranted, as we conceive, by virtue of that part of the constitution delegating *judicial power,* for the exercise of which any act of the legislature is provided, in exercising (even under the authority of another act) any power not in its nature judicial, or if judicial, *not provided for upon the terms the constitution requires.*

"*Fourthly :* That whatever doubts may be suggested, whether the power in question is properly of a judicial nature, yet inasmuch as the decision of the court is not made final, but may be, at least, suspended in its operation by the secretary at war, if he shall have cause to suspect imposition or mistake, this subjects the decision of the court to a mode of revision, which we consider to be unwarranted by the constitution : For, though Congress may certainly establish, in instances not yet provided for, courts of appellate jurisdiction ; yet, such courts must consist of judges appointed in the manner the constitution requires, and holding their offices by no other tenure than that of their good behaviour ; by which tenure the office of secretary at war is not held. And, we beg leave to add, with all due deference, that no decision of any court of the United States can, under any circumstances, in our opinion, agreeably to the constitution, be liable to a reversion, or even suspension, by the legislature itself, in whom no judicial power of any kind appears to be vested, but the important one relative to impeachments."

Extract from the opinion of *judges* WILSON, BLAIR, and PETERS.

"The people of the United States have vested in Congress all *legislative* powers, granted in the constitution.

"They have vested in one supreme court, and in such inferior courts as the Congress shall establish, the *judicial* power of the United States.

"It is worthy of remark, that, in Congress, the *whole* legislative power of the United States is not vested : an important part of that power was exercised by the people themselves, when they ' ordained and established the constitution.'

" This conftitution is the ' fupreme **law** of the land :' This fupreme law, ' all judicial officers of the United States are bound, by
oath or affirmation to fupport.'

" It is a principle important to freedom, that in government, the
judicial fhould be diftinct from, and independent of, the legiflative
department. To this important principle, the people of the United
States, in forming their conftitution, have manifefted the higheft
regard.

" They have placed their *judicial* power, not in Congrefs, but in
' courts.' They have ordained, that ' the judges' of thofe courts
fhall hold their offices during good behaviour ;' and that, ' during
their continuance in office, their falaries fhall not be diminifhed.'

" Congrefs have lately paffed an act ' to regulate (among other
things) the claims to invalid penfions.'

" Upon due **confideration**, we have been unanimoufly of opinion, that, under **this** act, **the circuit court, held** for the Pennfylvania
diftrict, could not proceed :

" *Firft*, Becaufe the bufinefs directed by this act, is not of a judicial nature. It forms no part of the power vefted by the conftitution
in the **courts** of the United States ; the circuit court muft, confequently, have proceeded without conftitutional authority.

" *Secondly*, Becaufe, if, upon that bufinefs, the court had proceeded ; *its judgments* (for its opinions are its judgments) *might,
under the fame act, have been revifed and controuled by the legiflature,
and by an officer in the executive department.* Such revifion and controul, we deemed radically inconfiftent **with the** independence of
that judicial power, **which** is vefted **in the courts ; and**, confequently,
with that important principle, which is fo ftrictly obferved by the
conftitution of the United States."

Extract from the opinion of *chief juftice* JAY, and *judges* CUSHING
and DUANE.

" The court were unanimoufly of opinion,

" *Firft*, That by the conftitution of the United States, the
government thereof is divided into *three* diftinct and independent
branches ; and, *that it is the duty of each to abftain from, and oppofe,
encroachments on either.*

" *Secondly*, That **neither the** *legiflative* nor *the executive branches,*
can conftitutionally affign **to** the *judicial* any duties, but fuch as are
properly judicial, and to be performed in a judicial manner.

" *Thirdly*, That the duties affigned to the circuit court by the act
in queftion, are not of that defcription ; and that the act itfelf does
not appear **to** contemplate them as fuch ; inafmuch as it fubjects the
decifion **of** thefe courts, made purfuant to thofe duties, firft to the
confideration and fufpenfion of the fecretary at war, and then to the
revifion of the legiflature ; *whereas, by the conftitution, neither the fecre-
ta y at war, nor any other executive officer, nor even the legiflature, are
authorifed to fit as a court of errors on the judicial acts or opinions of*
this court.

SUCH, upon the whole, are "*THE FEATURES OF MR. JAY'S TREATY.*" It was not intended to protract this sketch of them to so great a length; and yet, more circumstances are recollected, that might have been inserted, than could, upon a fair reconsideration, be retrenched. If it shall, in any degree serve the purposes of truth, by leading, through the medium of a candid investigation, *to a fair, honourable, and patriotic decision*, the design with which it was written will be completely accomplished, *whether RATIFICATION OR REJECTION is the result.*

But, before the subject is closed, let the citizens of the union be warned from too credulous an indulgence of *their prejudices* and *their fears.* The discordant cry of party is loud; and the phantoms of war assail the imagination: yet, let us not be deluded by stratagem, nor vanquished by terror. The question is not a question between party and party, but between nation and nation:—it is not a question of war or peace, between military powers; but a question of policy and interest between commercial rivals. The subject is too momentous, to be treated as the foot-ball of contending factions;—it appeals from the passions to the judgment; from the selfishness to the patriotism of every citizen!

That *the British treaty, or a British war, is a necessary alternative*, will be more fully controverted, if the writer's present intention of delineating "*FEATURES OF THE DEFENCE*," shall be carried into effect. But, in the mean time, let a few self-evident propositions contribute to relieve the public mind, from the weight of that apprehension.

1. The *disposition of Great Britain*, manifested by the order of the 6th of November, 1793, by the speech of Lord Dorchester to the Indians, and by the repeated invasions made, under General Simcoe's authority, upon our territory, *is naturally hostile to the United States.*

2. Even if the United States could, by any means, soothe and convert that disposition into amity and peace, *the projected treaty is too high a price to pay for such a change.*

3. The refusal to enter into the projected treaty with Great Britain, is *not a just cause of war*; and if a *pretence*, only, is wanting, it may be found in the toasts at our festivals, as well as in the acts of our government.

4. But the ratification of the treaty will assuredly give umbrage to *another nation*—to an ancient ally.

5. If war is inevitable *either with Great Britain, or with France*, it would be more politic for the state, more congenial to the sentiments of the people, to engage the former, than the latter, power.

6. In case of a war with Great Britain, we have assurance, *that France will aid us with all the energy of her triumphant arms.*

7. In case of a war with France, we ought not to count upon *the affections*, and we cannot rely upon the power, of Great Britain, to befriend us.

View of the Commerce of the United States, as it stands at present, and as it is fixed by Mr. Jay's Treaty.

1. *Actual State.*

AMERICAN ships from Europe enjoy a protecting duty of 10 per cent. on the amount of duties on goods, wares, and merchandiſes, imported into the United States in foreign bottoms from Europe, and of 30 to 50 per cent. on teas imported in foreign bottoms from Aſia or Europe, paid by foreign bottoms, more than is paid on ſuch goods imported in our own veſſels. Foreign bottoms pay alſo 44 cents a ton on every voyage, more than is paid by American ſhipping; all which had been allowed by the federal government, to encourage American ſhip-builders, mariners, mechanics, merchants, and farmers.

1. *State by Treaty.*

By treaty, America cedes to Great Britain, the right of laying duties on our ſhips in Europe, the Weſt Indies, and Aſia, to countervail theſe, and engages not to encreaſe her duties on tonnage on this ſide, ſo as to check the exerciſe of this right: in conſequence Britiſh ſhips may be put, at the diſcretion of the Britiſh government, on exactly the ſame footing, as American ſhips in the carrying trade of Europe and Aſia.

2. *Actual State.*

Americn ſhips, of any ſize, now go freely to all the Britiſh Weſt Indies, ſell their cargoes, and bring returns as it ſuits them.

2. *State by Treaty.*

By treaty American ſhips are to be reduced to *ſeventy tons,* in order to be admitted in the Britiſh Weſt Indies.

3. *Actual State.*

American ſhips may now freely load melaſſes, ſugar, coffee, cocoa, or cotton, to any part of the world from the United States.

3. *State by Treaty.*

By treaty American ſhips are to be totally prohibited this commerce, which is to be carried on under any flag but theirs.

4. *Actual State.*

American citizens can now go ſupercargoes to India, ſettle and reſide, and do their buſineſs there.

4. *State by Treaty.*

By treaty no American citizen can settle or reside in these ports, or go into the interior country, without special licence from the local government, who may, under colour of this, impose what obstacles they please to the commerce.

5. *Actual State.*

America now enjoys the right of regulating commerce, so as to encourage one nation and discourage another, in proportion to benefits received, or injuries felt respectively.

5. *State by Treaty.*

All this abandoned by the treaty so far as respects Great Britain ; no duties can be laid on British goods but what must apply to all other nations from whom we import goods—no embargoes on exports to British ports, but what must apply to all nations alike.

6. *Actual State.*

American ships now freely navigate to the British dominions in India, and from thence proceed with cargoes to any part of the world.

6. *State by Treaty.*

By treaty American ships are admitted as usual into the British ports of India, but prohibited carrying any return cargoes except to the United States; prohibited also from the coasting trade in the British ports of India, from which they were not, that I know of, before excluded.

7. *Actual State.*

Timber for ship-building, tar, or rozin, copper in sheets, sails, hemp, cordage, and generally whatever may serve directly to the equipment of vessels, not contraband by former treaties of the United States.

7. *State by Treaty.*

All these articles made contraband by this treaty.

8. *Actual State.*

American ships carrying provisions, by America claimed as having a free right of passage to the ports of their destination.

8. *State by Treaty.*

This claim now apparently waved ; such American ships, when taken, to be allowed indemnity of freight, demurrage, and a reasonable mercantile profit, the amount whereof not ascertained.

9. *Actual State.*

American ports open to prizes made on Britain by France ; and America possessed of the liberty to grant similar douceurs to other nations, as she sees fit in future compacts with them.

9. *State by Treaty.*

American ports now opened to prizes taken by Britain from any nation except France, but shut to prizes taken from Britain by Spain, or any other power not favoured in this way, by treaties already made ; of course discouraging to our future negociations with all powers, France and Britain excepted.

10. *Actual State.*

American ships allowed at prefent freely to enter British ports in Europe, the Weft Indies and Afia, but fhut out from the fea-ports of Nova-Scotia and Canada.

10. *State by Treaty.*

American fhips allowed to go into thefe ports, but under new reftrictions of fize, in the Weft Indies, and of latitude of trade in the Eaft Indies; the ports of Halifax, Quebec, &c. ftill fhut to America.

11. *Actual State.*

American fhips thus partially allowed entrance into British ports.

11. *State by Treaty.*

British fhips allowed univerfal entrance into all our ports.

12. *Actual State.*

American fhips now fail, though not under naval protection, under guarantee of all the British effects poffeffed here, which might be made anfwerable for our floating property, if unjuftly feized on by Great Britain in cafe of a war, fo much apprehended by the chamber of commerce of New-York.

12. *State by Treaty.*

By treaty, American fhips deprived of this guarantee; fequeftrations or confifcations being declared impolitic and unjuft, when applied to ftocks, or banks, or debts; though nothing faid about them when applied to fhips or cargoes.

13. *Actual State.*

British debts now recoverable in the federal courts of the United States, but repofing on the folvency of the debtors only.

13. *State by Treaty.*

By treaty a new court of commiffioners opened on this fubject, with immenfe power and guarantee of the United States, who muft meet, indeed, at Philadelphia, but may adjourn where they pleafe. Nothing faid of debts due to Americans in England, if, by legal impediments, prevented from recovery there.

14. *Actual State.*

America fends Mr. Jay to recover redrefs for fpoliations on our commerce actually fuftained.

14. *State by Treaty.*

By treaty a court of commiffioners opened, who are to fit in London without power of adjournment, as in the cafe of the commiffion for debts. Americans muft, therefore, tranfport themfelves and claims to London, and employ counfel there, to recover what the commiffioners fhall think fit to allow them: admirable compenfation indeed!

15. *Actual State.*

American fhips much plagued by British privateers.

15. *State by Treaty.*

By treaty the privateerfmen are to give 15,ool. to 300ol. fterling fecurity for their **good** behaviour.

16. *Actual State.*

American citizens may now expatriate and serve in foreign countries.

16. *State by Treaty.*

By treaty they are declared pirates, if serving against Great Britain; but no provision made to guard American seaman from being forced to serve in British ships.

17. *Actual State.*

America possesses claims to a large amount on account of negroes carried off, and the Western Posts detained, in violation of the treaty of 1783.

17. *State by Treaty.*

These claims all waved by the treaty, without reference to the merits of these pretensions.

The casting up of the above, is submitted to the Chamber of Commerce of New-York.

Errors, outstandings, and omissions excepted.

Philadelphia, July 27, 1795.

FINIS.

www.ingramcontent.com/pod-product-compliance
Lightning Source LLC
Chambersburg PA
CBHW022201020726
47496CB00008B/2824